THE NEW DEMOCRACY AND THE CONSTITUTION

THE NEW DEMOCRACY AND THE CONSTITUTION

By WILLIAM SHARP McKECHNIE

KENNIKAT PRESS
Port Washington, N. Y./London

THE NEW DEMOCRACY AND THE CONSTITUTION

First published in 1912
Reissued in 1971 by Kennikat Press
Library of Congress Catalog Card No: 71-118485
ISBN 0-8046-1234-X

Manufactured by Taylor Publishing Company Dallas, Texas

TO

E. C. M.

CONTENTS

INTRODUCTION

DEMOCRACY AS A WORKING SCHEME OF GOVERNMENT

CHAPTER I

ANCIENT CONSTITUTIONAL LANDMARKS AS MODIFIED BY MODERN DEMOCRATIC THEORIES

CHAPTER II

THE CONSTITUTION OF TO-DAY COMPARED WITH THE CONSTITUTION OF FIFTY YEARS AGO

CHAPTER III

TENDENCIES OF MODERN DEMOCRATIC LEGISLATION

CHAPTER IV

THE STUMBLING BLOCKS OF DEMOCRACY

CHAPTER V

THE THEORETICAL BASIS OF DEMOCRACY

CHAPTER VI

SAFEGUARDS AND PRACTICAL SUGGESTIONS

THE NEW DEMOCRACY AND THE CONSTITUTION

INTRODUCTION

DEMOCRACY AS A WORKING SCHEME OF GOVERNMENT

If professions of politicians mean anything, the triumph of Democracy in Great Britain is now assured. The proof lies in the line of argument habitually adopted by both parties in all the great controversies of the day, and especially conspicuous throughout the constitutional crisis that culminated in the Parliament Act of 1911. A fervent and almost servile eagerness to interpret and to execute "the people's will" is as persistently proclaimed by Conservatives and Liberals as by Socialists and Labour leaders. These earnest and unanimous professions must be accepted as genuine. No sincere reformer would dare to repudiate the principle now accepted as self-evident that government "of the people, by the people, for the people" is the sole rule of progress and humanity. For

Liberals the battle sternly fought and now finally won has been throughout that of the people against the peers: the present Constitution of 1911, embodying this triumph, has, in its promoters' eyes, the one great merit that under it in future "the will of the people" always must prevail. The citadels of class-privilege have been stormed and destroyed.

Conservative statesmen, on the other hand, whether peers or commoners, have been equally emphatic that their main object in resisting the Parliament Bill has been to protect the people from being balked of their real desires by the Chamber of their own election. The ancient powers of the House of Lords have been defended by Conservatives almost exclusively on the ground that they ensured the triumph of the genuine "will of the people" against a capricious, selfish, or obsolescent House of Commons. The strongest argument for the Referendum takes a similar trend: the best method of giving effect to the sacred "will of the people" is to refer each legislative measure separately to the decision of the citizens voting an explicit "yes" or "no" on each particular issue as it arises.

No real difference remains as to the guiding postulate of modern politics. The statesman's duty is summed up in one sentence: "Find what the people want, and see that they get it." This profession of belief, once publicly made, cannot lightly be withdrawn. Anyone who has ever stood on a modern election platform can readily imagine the spasm of dismay that would pass over the sea of listening faces, if a candidate declared his distrust in the perfect justice, wisdom, and moderation of "the people." The favours of King Demos are to be won like those of other kings; the flattery may be coarser and may take a form more practical, but flattery there must be. The unvarnished truth is never well received at Court. It follows that a cordial acquiescence in what is willed by the people for the present and for the future must continue to guide the utterances of all who knock at the carefully guarded doors of the Representative Chamber. At future elections, as at both those of 1910, candidates will make it plain that, however deeply they may distrust either or both Houses of Parliament, however they may suspect the leaders of all or any of the great political parties; they yet place implicit confidence in the sovereign people. This spirit of meek prostration before "the people's will" is the quintessence of modern Democracy. This modern Democracy is not the limited democracy of the past, tempered by the survival of counterbalancing royal and hereditary influences that once formed prominent ingredients in the admired "mixed Constitution" as known to

Blackstone and De Lolme, but a democracy free to use to the uttermost, powers that are absolute and unchecked.

This change from a qualified to an unqualified sovereignty of the people involves a momentous shifting of the political centre of gravity. To analyse the direction and nature of this change is the main object of these essays. Meanwhile, it is accepted as axiomatic that in all circumstances and at all costs the will of the people must prevail.

I. *Underlying Principles of Democracy.*

Not all who acquiesce in the formulas of popular government have analysed what is involved in the attempt to carry them consistently into practice. It is easier to invoke or to deplore democracy than to say exactly what it is. For some of its adherents, it takes the negative form of a protest against luxury and class privilege; for others it takes the positive form of a scheme for turning England, or the whole world, into a poor man's paradise. To some, its economic aspects, to others, its political possibilities make the deeper appeal.

Vague platitudes will not help the inquiry. Democracy, when the term is strictly used, is a system of government—the reign of the people—of the many as opposed to the one or the few. This does not imply that the people in their multitudes actually lay hands on the reins of office; but merely that their collective will (found through the simple process of adding and subtracting individual votes) has absolute though indirect control over those who actually perform the functions of government. Democracy, as popular control, is thus something widely different from mere mob-rule, or even from systems involving the rotation of power, or its determination by the drawing of lots. Democracy, in brief, means a system of government which ensures that the people's will prevails. The question thus presses for an answer: What practical consequences are likely to result from acceptance of this maxim followed by a sincere attempt to carry it out consistently to its logical results?

(1) *Universal Suffrage.*—In theory, no democrat can be a respecter of persons. One human being is as good as another. That hitherto elastic term "the people" must be elastic no longer; but, stretched to its utmost extent, it must be fixed there against all possibility of recoil. No one can be arbitrarily excluded from full citizenship. Lunatics, indeed, may be permanently disfranchised on the ground that they are not "persons"; and children, temporarily, as not having yet attained to that full status. Condemned criminals, also,

while actually serving their term of sentence may, perhaps, also be debarred from voting, though not without some violence to the logic of a democratic theory which grants equal citizenship to the unfit as to the fit. But, at that point, the legitimate limits of exclusion have been reached. A democracy cannot reject anyone on grounds of sex, rank, race, or economic disabilities. Illiterates, paupers, and those suffering from physical or mental defects, short of absolute insanity, must be freely admitted; while aliens, however undesirable, can be rejected only with some violence to strict consistency. Women clearly can only be excluded on arguments utterly undemocratic.

A practical democracy, on the other hand, is limited to those actually alive at the moment its sovereign wishes are consulted. Posterity has no direct voice and no accredited representatives in the councils of democracy, which thus falls short of Edmund Burke's definition of the ideal commonwealth as "a partnership not only between those who are living, but between those who are living, those who are dead, and those who are to be born."

(2) *Equality.*—Absolute equality in the rights and duties of citizenship is obviously an essential of a true democracy. Not only must the portals of the ideal commonwealth be open to all, but every one who has entered must, irrespective

of the worth of his contribution to its welfare, enjoy an equal vote in the shaping of its destinies. Conservative statesmen, at the present moment, are even more vehement than their rivals in insisting on the absolute necessity of the equal values of individual votes. Both parties, in their eager service of the people, are agreed, so far as their public utterances go, that each voter, without respect to moral, intellectual, or property qualifications, ought to enjoy exactly the same microscopical fraction of control over the national policy.

Politicians still differ widely as to the ideal size of electoral areas, as to the competing claims of single, double, or multiplex constituencies, as to the ballot or the open poll, as to the rival merits of the present system as opposed to the cumulative or the single transferable vote; but no thorough-going democrat dares to question the necessity of erasing utterly all vestiges of inequality. The unfair preference given to property owners by the plural vote must go; the unfair preference given to education, as embodied in the representation of universities, must go; the unfair disabilities imposed on paupers and those unable to pay poor-rates must also go; the disfranchisement effected by the present registration system can no longer be endured. Sincere democratic sentiment will tolerate nothing short of universal equal suffrage without respect of age, sex, or rank in life. In this view, it is absurd that 53,000 electors of the Romford division of Essex should only have one member to represent them, while 2600 citizens of Durham should have a member to themselves. Here one voter of the latter constituency is made of equal value with twenty of the former. This is an outrage on the sacred principle of equality.

The immediate establishment of absolutely equal electoral areas and a considered scheme for their continual readjustment to meet fluctuations of population are then among the most urgent objects of democratic statesmanship. Absolute equality, irrespective of moral worth, of services to the community, or of fitness for civic life, is the fundamental principle of democratic theory.

(3) *Closer Control by the Electorate over the Government.*—Representatives and governments are placed in power not to forward their own schemes but to obey the orders of their masters: the people's control can never be too close, constant, or inquisitorial. On democratic principles, it ought therefore to be impossible to withhold adherence to four expedients (on which, however, opinion is by no means uniform at the present moment), namely, the doctrine of the "mandate," short parliaments, the "recall,"[1] and the Referendum with its corollary the Initiative. In the United States a fifth appli-

[1] The nature of the "recall" is explained, *infra*, p. 11.

cation of the principle of popular control has found general acceptance; for there the judges of various States are appointed by popular election.

If any one finds himself unable to accept these principles in their entirety, he has cause to reconsider his position; for assuredly he is no whole-hearted democrat. Lord Morley, indeed, has recently declared against the "mandate," on the ground that "the standard of always consulting and being guided by and thinking of nothing else but what the people desire is to my mind a thoroughly wrong standard. . . . What Ministers and Legislative Houses ought to be considering is what they believe is for the good government of the country"[1]; but this merely proves that Lord Morley is an intellectual aristocrat, fundamentally out of sympathy with modern democracy, and still clinging to the older so-called representative government, now discredited with advanced reformers.

Statesmen of Lord Morley's moral fibre are by no means the only opponents of the mandate: for that doctrine is extremely inconvenient to those who profess lip service to the wishes of the people, and yet despise or fear them in their hearts. Both Houses of Parliament are

[1] *Vide* Debate on Lord Balfour's Reference to the People Bill, 28th March 1911.

only too ready with their rival claims to interpret the tacit commands of the people; but surely the people know best themselves what they really want. The doctrine of the mandate, in its positive and negative aspects alike, is a necessary article in the democratic creed.

Frequent elections are equally essential. Quinquennial parliaments are too independent of their constituents. A voter's desires and aims may alter radically in five years (or indeed in five days): and it is monstrous that he should be compelled to sit in silence, while the individual he has voted for acts in the elector's name against the elector's wishes. The people have a perfect right to be fickle, if they please. Theoretically, therefore, elections cannot occur too frequently. Yet practical considerations — expenditure of labour, time, and money, need of stability, and so forth—render weekly or monthly elections impossible, and even annual elections of doubtful desirability. The common sense of democratic leaders is sorely taxed to adjust the divergent details of theory and practice, yet long parliaments, however the adjective may be defined, stand condemned.

Further, if a Member deliberately opposes the wishes of his constituents, some rapid method of dissolving the tie between them must be found. It is obviously absurd that any section of the sovereign people should be openly flouted by the agent, now the paid agent, appointed to register its commands. No sensible tradesman would conduct his business on such lines. Even apart from dishonesty or incapacity, it is intolerable that a popular nominee should show any slackness in opposing a measure to which the effective majority of his constituents object. Yet, in spite of the Parliament Act of 1911, the hands of electors may still be tied for the best part of five years. Constitutional machinery ought to be provided, in a real democracy, for the immediate dismissal of a discredited representative. This is the principle of "the recall" which Mr Ellis F. Powell, in a recent work on *The Essentials of Self-Government*, argues, with irresistible logic, to be essential to any real control by the people over their own destinies. In each constituency must be vested "the sole and uninterrupted right of dismissing a member." The main steps in the necessary procedure are in Mr Powell's opinion two: a primary requisition for his resignation by 10 per cent. of his constituents, followed, after a due interval for investigations and other safeguards, by a final requisition to the same effect by 55 per cent., whereupon the seat becomes vacant.[1] He insists on this right of dismissal as marking off real "self-government" from the older system

[1] Pages 277-291. *Cf.* p. 2.

of "representative government." If Mr Powell's logical conclusions can be upset, it is certainly not by those who argue on democratic premises.

(4) *The Referendum.*—A similar line of argument leaves consistent adherents of a pure democracy no loophole of escape from the principle of the Referendum. If the people are really fit to rule, they are fit to pronounce sentence on the details of all bills before they become law. They must not be deceived by those in power.

A short historical digression will illustrate this danger. The first step towards the Commons' control over legislation was taken in the reign of Henry V., when their prayer was granted that statutes should not be passed except in the exact form of the petitions they had presented. Previously monarchs had often played dishonest tricks upon them by manipulating the terms of the petition. The change marked a new step from autocratic to representative government. The advance from the latter to real self-government as defined by its advocates, demands an equally effective check upon the practices of modern parliaments. The voters must be able to satisfy themselves that they are not having foisted on them measures essentially different from those they want. In only one way can this be effected, namely: by the Referendum. In this respect at least, the bulk of Conservative statesmen are better democrats than the bulk of Liberals.

The weighty arguments sometimes urged against the Referendum are, on the accepted hypothesis, irrelevant. To maintain that the sovereign people are too ignorant or too preoccupied with other duties, too selfish or too unjust to be trusted to decide the details of numerous bills, is not to attack the Referendum as one instrument of democracy, but rather to attack democracy itself.

The principle of the Referendum must be frankly accepted by all consistent advocates of pure democracy. In theory at least the more frequently it is used, the more complete will be the approximation to an ideal form of government on the accepted hypothesis. In this respect, the compulsory Referendum is more democratic than the voluntary or "facultative" form, as both are known in modern Switzerland. Even in that cradle of direct popular legislation, financial measures have been withdrawn—apparently from a lurking disbelief in the complete wisdom or integrity of the people—from the operation of the Referendum, a concession wrung from the logic of theory by the harder logic of facts. In April 1891, however, the Swiss Commonwealth adopted the logical supplement of the Referendum, namely, the "Initiative," which confers on any 50,000 individual voters the right to frame (in rivalry with the official legislature) bills of their own, to compel a reference of these bills to a mass vote of the whole nation, and in the event of a favourable popular verdict to force them on to the Statute Book in defiance of the warnings and adverse votes of both Houses of their Parliament. There are thus two methods of legislating in Switzerland. A measure may be introduced in Parliament, and after receiving the support of both Houses, it is in the normal case still subject to a "veto" by a popular Referendum. If a bill is introduced by the popular "Initiative," however, the rights of veto of both Houses of the Legislature are absolutely abolished, not merely that of the Upper Chamber, as in England of the Parliament Act.

Drastic as this interference with Parliament's authority may seem, there can be no question of its conformity to democratic ideals. Great Britain will remain a home of aristocratic privilege as compared with progressive Switzerland, unless it adopts, along with the Swiss Referendum, the Swiss "Initiative," which would allow the people directly (when they chose) to make their own laws, and would thus reduce the House of Commons to a condition of impotence, in which it would become as powerless to betray the people's trust by vetoing the people's wishes, as the House of Lords has already become under the Parliament Act. Thus, on democratic principles, the Referendum and Initiative, like the "recall," the "mandate," and all the other devices for subjecting the legislature to the domination of the people, cannot be set aside. To oppose the acceptance of any one of these nostrums, even in its most drastic form, is to qualify the principles of pure democracy by antagonistic principles; to reinstate old-fashioned constitutional maxims, which *ex hypothesi* must be discarded.

II. *Divergence between the Theory and Practice of Democracy.*

The democracy of abstract theory, it is commonly argued, differs materially from the democracy of actual practice. It is necessary to face this possibility, and to estimate as far as may be the nature, extent, and direction of such divergence.

The doctrine of equality is sometimes declared to be founded on illusion. However great the care taken to secure an identical fraction of voting power to each voting atom, all real authority will tend to concentrate in the hands of a few. The nature and title to power of the ruling aristocracy will be changed; and that is all. The extent of this process of concentration will vary with the character of every age and nation, and even with the circumstances of each successive election.

Crowds are liable to be swayed by eloquence: individuals to be influenced by ties of friendship, or by deference to the opinions of others. The actual vote of the individual member of a free commonwealth comes to be of trivial importance compared with the extent of his influence over the votes of others. The man of position, wealth, or moral worth, or above all of subtle intellect and effective oratory may command hundreds or thousands of votes. A nominal equality, it is urged, by no means results in the triumph of sheer brute numbers over the finer and subtler influences that build up a nation's greatness. Under a free democracy there is infinite room for delicate adjustments, and every form of social virtue, every quality that has value for the furtherance of the national welfare, will carry precisely the weight to which it is entitled and which is most likely to do good. The equality of the doctrinaire gives way, before the logic of actuality, to a scale of power graded according to individual and social merit.

Students of politics, of a less optimistic type, draw a different picture. In their view, power over the equal votes of the many does not naturally gravitate to those who, by their wisdom, benevolence, and truthfulness, are best able to use it for the public welfare; but rather to those who do not scruple to obtain it by adroit cajolery, suppression of unwelcome truths, and promises of reward. The reign of King Demos is not necessarily a state of society in which the highest and enduring interests of the commonwealth are entrusted to those best fitted for the task, but rather the triumph of those who sacrifice the future to the present, the minority to the majority, and the provident and self-reliant to the wastrel and malingerer. In the opinion of such prophets of evil, open flattery and veiled bribery are the surest methods of gaining the popular influence which is now the only road to political power.

The divergence between theory and practice may thus be used for their own purposes by the friends and enemies of equality in turn. This possibility in no way militates against the theory of democracy, which leaves every man free to use his vote in his own way. If an ignorant elector follows the interested advice of a glib-tongued trickster, or defers to the wishes of one he considers wiser than himself, he still votes for what he wants, just as much as though he were guided solely by his own appetites or passions. He still makes his individual contribution to the national will, equally with the elector who has deeply studied the science of politics, or with him who is ready to support the first candidate who offers him a motor ride to the place of polling. The deferential A has an equal right to mould the policy of the nation as has the opinionative and self-centred B. The tendency of masses to follow popular leaders blindly is by no means inconsistent with a doctrine that takes no account of inequalities. Democratic ideals must not be pronounced unrealisable because the postulated static equality turns in action to a dynamic inequality.

Under this proviso, four aspects of these disturbing forces call for brief comment:—(1) The influence of political organisations; (2) the pressure of trade unions; (3) the legislative authority of the House of Commons; (4) the control exercised by the Cabinet.

(1) *The Influence of Political Organisations.*—Votes recorded for a candidate with no chance of success are simply thrown away. Under normal conditions, only official candidates can possibly succeed. Organisation is thus required to prevent the "sovereign will of the people" dissipating itself in useless eccentricities; everything depends on the decisions of the party wirepullers. No candidate can obtain a hearing, no grievance however crying has a chance of redress, unless pushed by a properly constituted authority.

Individual votes then are captured and controlled by political associations. The sweet simplicity of "one man one vote" is engulfed in the whirlpools of the party caucus. The millions of voters become mere pawns in a game controlled by complex forces in which political ambition, intellect, wealth, and persuasive eloquence play leading rôles. The will of the effective majority tends to be the will of a political organisation, and that in turn is determined partly by the character and inclination of the few outstanding politicians who, by gaining the ear of the multitude, have got themselves accepted as party leaders; partly by the conditions laid down by subscribers to the party war-chest; and partly by the necessity of an attractive electioneering programme. The vital question for democracies comes to be whether the masses will adhere to leaders able and ready to lead them in the paths of economic soundness and moral rectitude, or to those who are willing to gamble with the fate of nations; and to advance their own careers by inflaming the popular passions it is their duty to allay.

(2) *The Action of Trade Unions.*—Among the agencies that disturb the theoretical equality of the distribution of political authority, the most potent are perhaps those formed for industrial rather than political objects. Trade unions are intended to promote the interests of the men employed in a particular industry, and not the interests of the nation as a whole: the two sets of interests, indeed, are often

sharply opposed. There is nothing unfair in this; but, all the same, it is a menace to the well-being of the community, that organisations with interests antagonistic to its own, should gain an ever-increasing control over the national destinies. If the machinery of the State—the Parliament and the Executive—come to obey the behests of bodies frankly concentrating their energies on the furtherance of their own selfish interests, it is evident that all rival interests must necessarily suffer. Industrial organisations, able to bring effective pressure on the Government, through their control over the massed votes of their own members, will put an end to the equality on which a pure democracy is in theory founded.

The force of this disturbing influence is increased by more than one notable tendency of modern political conditions; by the efforts made by trade unions to compel unwilling members to pay for political purposes of which they disapprove, and by the skilful manner in which official parliamentary action to alter the law for the future is combined with unofficial attempts, in time of strikes, to defy the operation of the existing law. Legal principles, for which no precedents can be found on our Statute Rolls, were embodied in an Act of Parliament in 1906 at the dictation of trade unions, in opposition to the settled opinions of a majority of both

Houses of Parliament, and after they had been deliberately rejected by the responsible government of the day. Where laws partial to labour cannot be peaceably obtained, strikes accompanied by acts of violence and intimidation are resorted to.

By skilful tactics in the employment of their always increasing powers, trade unions are thus enabled to paralyse the arm of the law, to compel partial legislation, and to prevent the untrammelled expression of the genuine will of the people. The pressure of such organisations is one of the methods which tend to substitute interests for principles as the guiding star of modern political life.

(3) *The Legislative Authority of the House of Commons.*—The sovereign people do not directly make laws for themselves, but merely appoint from time to time those who do. The concurrence of the King, still theoretically necessary to all statutes, and that of the House of Lords to non-financial bills, are now of little moment; since the Commons by the Parliament Act of 1911 have practically made good their claims to legislative omnipotence. During the life of a quinquennial Parliament, the nominal powers of many millions of citizens are exercised without legal control by their 670 elected representatives. These Members of Parliament, however, while unshackled by legal restraints, are by no

means free agents, politically and morally. They are not at liberty to vote according to their judgment of what is wise or unwise, right or wrong. They move under a double bondage to their election pledges and to the party Whips.

The extent to which the People's Chamber is dominated by outside influences, however, does not modify the fact that the people use their power not directly but only through their nominees. When all is said, the individual Member of Parliament has a greater share of legislative power than any one of the constituents who elect him. Here, again, practical necessities stultify the boast of democracy that all citizens enjoy an equality of political power.

(4) *The Authority exercised by the Cabinet over the Electorate.*—Since the Reform Act of 1867, statesmen have been constrained to take the nation more closely into confidence. By the promulgation of party programmes and by the practice of stump oratory, modern Cabinet leaders have been brought into more intimate touch with the electorate. They have thus drawn to themselves much of the popular favour formerly divided less unequally among the members of the Lower Chamber, and have, in doing so, increased their control over the parliamentary machine. The initiative and independence lost by the rank and file of individual members have gone to swell the

authority of the Cabinet. That Cabinet has appropriated for its own measures practically the whole time of the House available for legislation. It habitually rules the party majority, on whose favour it is nominally dependent, with a rod of iron, and hustles through Parliament by means of the "guillotine" whatever measures it pleases, half-discussed or not discussed at all.

Much of the tremendous power of the giant Democracy, so far from remaining evenly distributed among the constituent atoms, is thus, for effective purposes, concentrated in the fifteen or twenty politicians who from time to time compose the Cabinet. Concentration does not necessarily stop even here: if one man by his pre-eminent favour with the masses, makes himself indispensable to the Government's retention of office, he can by threat of resignation force upon his colleagues any measures or amendments on which he has set his heart. Whether a Cabinet is dominated by one man or by a group of men, it is clear that the supreme power which in democratic theory ought to be equally shared by all, is in practice monopolised by the Ministry so long as that Ministry retains the confidence of the House of Commons. The Oligarchy of Officials, indeed, rests on the Democracy and must humour it. If it can feed King Demos with the property of rival oligarchies, then it will continue to enjoy the prestige and emoluments of office; to favour its supporters; and to punish the opponents of its policy, by one and the same expedient.

III. *The Seat of Sovereignty.*

The encroachments made in practice by the House of Commons on the rights of the sovereign people, and by the Cabinet on the rights of the House of Commons, cannot be fully appreciated without some discussion of the seat of "Sovereignty" (or supreme power in the State) under the modern British Constitution. The accepted doctrine would seem to be that while "political sovereignty" lies with the mass of the electors, "legal or legislative sovereignty" lies with the King in Parliament.

In light of the foregoing analysis, it may seem preferable to use a different formula: while, in democratic doctrine, "sovereignty" lies with "the people" considered as a sum of equal units; under the modern British Constitution, as it works in practice, sovereignty is divided between the electorate, the House of Commons, and the Cabinet: but the latter, if it knows its business, secures the lion's share. Whatever the Cabinet wants—within certain limits at least—will in time become the law of the land. Thus in normal circumstances, the Cabinet is sovereign;

but if that Cabinet passes the undefined limits; the Legislature, worm as it is, may turn, or the electorate, favoured by the accident of numerous by-elections or in the throes of a general election, may dismiss one Ministry and appoint another to act as legal sovereign until the next crisis arrives.

"Sovereignty" in Great Britain at the present day would thus seem to have three different meanings. At the moment of a general election the electorate are sovereign, for on their votes depends the choice of rulers. The moment the election is over, the Commons, with the so-called vetoes of King and Upper Chamber reduced to impotence, enjoy in theory the sovereignty. But the proved impossibility of any bills but those of Ministers becoming law, bestows that sovereignty in practice upon the Cabinet, so long as it remains in office. This doctrine of a shifting sovereignty is obviously in direct contradiction to the orthodox theory of John Austin, who believed in a fixed sovereignty, and held that that sovereignty must in every State be permanently vested for all purposes in the same organ of government. The Austinian theory, however, long disputed in its applicability to such constitutions as that of the United States of America, must, like other theories, be prepared to bow to facts.

Under the British Constitution, as moulded

by recent events, the undivided supreme power always lies with one or other of the two parties that divide the State. However that sovereignty may shift from Cabinet to Commons or from Commons to electorate, no tiniest fraction of it can ever be shared by the defeated party—the party of minorities; for that party has been outvoted at the polls, is habitually outvoted in the Commons, and is entirely unrepresented in the Cabinet. Sovereignty in fact lies with the leaders of the dominant party: the same knot of politicians who control the Commons, likewise control the Cabinet. They also are mainly instrumental in forming the opinions of the rank and file of their party.

Democracy, far from embodying compromise, implies a monopoly of power by one-half of the people over the other half. Each party in turn is absolutely supreme, without let or hindrance. Sovereignty is no longer divided between King, Lords, and Commons, but is concentrated in the leaders of the party in power, on the one condition that they continue to lead. This is the fundamental fact to be kept in view in any analysis of the British Constitution of to-day. Such an analysis is attempted in the following six chapters which will proceed to discuss:—(1) How far the old historic landmarks of English constitutional development have been obliterated; (2) the main points of difference between the Palmerstonian Constitution as it was described by Bagehot and the Constitution as it stands to-day; (3) the probable effects of democratic legislation on the future of the British Constitution and of the British race; (4) possible dangers of democracy; (5) the soundness of the historic and philosophic basis of democratic theory; (6) the desirability of devising safeguards for the rights of minorities in the future, and the directions in which these are likely to be found.

The problems involved are of wider range and more lasting importance than the controversies that centred round the passing of the Parliament Act. They touch the foundations of the State, on which all parties find common foothold; and it ought to be possible to approach them with comparatively open minds, free from the heat engendered by the arrogance of victory or the bitterness of defeat.

CHAPTER I

ANCIENT CONSTITUTIONAL LANDMARKS AS MODIFIED BY MODERN DEMOCRATIC THEORIES

UNBROKEN continuity of development has been the dominating characteristic of British institutions in the past. Will the advent of democracy involve a breach of continuity? Is it necessary to abandon essential principles of a system of government admired and copied by all freedom-loving nations? "The unanimous judgment of the world at the beginning of the twentieth century," says Professor G. B. Adams of Yale,[1] the latest of a long line of distinguished commentators on our Constitution, "is that this is the best system of government yet devised. . . . The English Constitution has made the circuit of the globe and become the common possession of civilised man. After so many centuries of experiment, practical action, whatever be the opinion of the theorist, unites to declare this the best result of all experience."

In attempting to determine how far it is

[1] *Origin of the English Constitution* (1912), p. 1.

possible for this historic English Constitution to adapt itself to the needs of a democratic age without impairing its identity, it will be necessary to pass in brief review the chief features of that Constitution, as these have been known to its commentators from Blackstone to Professor Dicey. This will involve a brief discussion of (1) the nature of representative government; (2) the composition and authority of the Representative Chamber; (3) the connection between taxation and representation; (4) the theory of parliamentary finance; (5) the attitude of the Legislature towards private property; (6) the relations between supply and the redress of grievances; (7) the doctrine of the distribution of powers, or the Constitution considered as a system of checks and balances.

I. *Representative Government.*

If one feature more than another has been associated with the growth of constitutional liberty in England, it is the principle of representative government. The responsibility of Crown Ministers to Parliament has been, since the Revolution of 1688, the essence of that English polity which has set the fashion for all progressive nations. The English people have never — not even during the ferment of the Commonwealth — attempted to rule directly;

they have been content to rule through representatives in whose wisdom and integrity they believed. Parliamentary government, as hitherto practised in Great Britain, has differed widely from self-government in the strictest sense; for the electors have never dictated the details of legislation or interfered directly with the work of administration. Recent writers have shown a tendency to draw a sharp distinction between real self-government, as they define it, and the older form of government by representatives.[1]

The classic exposition of the ideals of the ancient system must still be sought in the famous words addressed by Edmund Burke to his constituents at Bristol.[2] "Your representative owes you, not his industry only, but his judgment, and he betrays, instead of serving you, if he sacrifices it to your opinion." Since Burke's day, all this has been changed. The modern House of Commons is no longer made up of free representatives, but of tied delegates, fettered by definite promises made before election, to which they are forced to adhere by pressure of the party Whips. Acknowledging the doctrine of the mandate, and pledged on every important issue long before debate upon it has begun, they are reduced to casting a mechanical vote without possibility of giving effect to such modifications

[1] See *e.g.* Mr Powell's view, cited *suprâ*, p. 11.

[2] *Works*, ii., 19.

of preconceived ideas, as new arguments and the disclosure of new facts demand. The House of Commons is no longer what it once was, a flexible assembly, open to conviction, capable of altering its decisions as altering circumstances suggest. When it was all this, it exercised a healthy supervision over the conduct of Ministers; it lived, in Walter Bagehot's happy phrase, "in a condition of perpetual potential choice." Swayed by the course of debate, it indicated by the fluctuations of each division, the measure in which its confidence waxed or waned. No Ministry was so secure, but that at any moment, an unforeseen catastrophe might turn it adrift.

The change is now complete. A Prime Minister in the twentieth century may count on the automatic support of the serried ranks of a parliamentary majority pledged beforehand to the party programme. He is thus relieved from the wholesome restraint that leads to moderation. Government by the parliamentary machine has supplanted, or will soon supplant, government by free discussion. The effective majority of the Lower House has become the unreasoning tool of the Cabinet's will, instead of its critic and master. Representative government of the type known to Burke, Fox, or Pitt, to Canning, Peel, or Palmerston, to Gladstone or Disraeli, has given way to government by the party machine voting to order. Many of the favourite expedients for effecting reforms at the present day, such as the doctrine of the mandate, the Referendum and Initiative, the need of shorter parliaments, and the right to dismiss off-hand a discredited representative, would accelerate this process of change from the older theory to the new. Great Britain is rapidly progressing from representative government to self-government in the stricter, more modern meaning of the term.

II. *Changes in Representative Chamber.*

The general body of electors cannot take the reins into their own hands. Agents of some kind they must have, whether real representatives or tied delegates. Under any system of self-government, a Representative Chamber of some sort must exist. The House of Commons, as at present constituted, is the result of a long process of development; and the relations of the House to the electors have altered greatly in the last half century, if not in the last decade. In view of recent developments, it is not unnatural to ask to what extent Parliament is still representative of the various factors that go to the making of Great Britain.

No Chamber can be a real epitome of English life, if it does not reproduce in their due proportions the elements that together constitute the English nation. Unfortunately, the factors that contribute to a country's prosperity are unequally distributed throughout the population. Some of the most valuable qualities are the heritage of the few. A chamber elected exclusively on the basis of population, of quantity divorced from quality, cannot be really an epitome of the nation. All the complex features that distinguish Great Britain from other nations ought to find due place in a truly British Parliament. The House of Commons, speaking proudly in England's name, must see that it is really a microcosm of English life and of English ideals and achievements.

The historical traditions of Great Britain, her advance in commercial enterprise, invention, and material prosperity, her contributions to science, art, and literature, her success as a colonising power and as a ruler of dependencies, her achievement in naval and military activities, the extent to which the happiness, health, and moral worth of her citizens have been realised—all these are joint products of the interaction of various forces—not of the unrestrained predominance of the will of the numerical majority. Industry, foresight, property, social eminence, eloquence, power of leadership, agriculture, manufacture, trade, philanthropy, moral energy, and religious fervour, have all helped to build up the national character in ratios that vary out of all proportion to the actual numerical voting power of the individuals in whom they are found. A really national Parliament, whether of one or of two chambers, ought to blend in due proportions representatives of labour, capital, rank, ability, mental and moral eminence, as well as of numbers pure and simple.

Until late in the nineteenth century, the Lower Chamber was viewed as an assembly of the representatives of corporate groups, whether towns or counties, rather than as representing the common or ordinary people as a whole. For over five centuries, each pair of members had represented primarily the corporate local interests of Bristol or of Kent, rather than those of several thousands of isolated and equal voters. The very anomalies of the old borough franchise, however unjust and indefensible, had the merit of securing that minorities of various types were not altogether unrepresented in the House: an approximation was made to the ideal of Burke that "the virtue, spirit, and essence of a House of Commons, consists in its being the express image of the feelings of a nation."[1] Each pair of members then represented one of the complex little groups in which the national life concentrated.

The theory of representation has suffered

[1] *Works*, ii., 288.

change. Insidiously the new conception has gained ground that Parliament should represent numbers and nothing else.

The franchise is no longer viewed as something that ought to be confined to those best able to use it for the common weal, but as a right to be conceded to all who insist on having it. It is no longer regarded as a public trust, but as a weapon to be used for selfish individual ends. The formula of "one man one vote" is supplemented by that of "one vote, one value," and the most meticulous care of reformers is directed towards the scrupulous calculation of exact equality in the fractional values of individual votes. Constant revision is demanded to secure that for all political purposes the educated and the ignorant should rank alike. The ideal House of Commons of the future, purged of all complexity and anomalies, will be absolutely homogeneous in composition. The will of the people will then be ascertained by a huge sum in addition.

Such are the various aspects of the new theory of representation, now accepted by all active politicians: any expressed doubt of the axiom, indeed, would involve an immediate exclusion from political life. These beliefs, or pretences of belief, have ripened gradually, until they have now become an indispensable part of ordinary thought and language. The extent to which they involve a radical break with the past seems to have been insufficiently recognised.

Some theorists, indeed, deny that a House of Commons elected under democratic ideals would represent merely the brute voting power of numbers. On the contrary, they affirm, it is precisely under a system of universal suffrage that the various factors in national prosperity obtain their proper weight. These factors exercise, it is argued, a potent indirect influence. Motives both good and evil are said to contribute to this result. The inherent snobbery of human nature leads the obscure and needy to defer to the wishes of the rich and fashionable; while millions of voters may be swayed by the wisdom and eloquence of a few brilliant individuals. All influences that tend to differentiate between the theory and practice of democracy will combine, it is argued, to make a Parliament elected by popular suffrage really representative of everything that is best and most characteristic in the nation. The masses of half-educated voters are looked upon as so much malleable material to be hammered into shape by the agencies that play upon them.

To those who accept this view, the nominal equality of voting power allows in practice the free play of all the varied forces that make for inequality. The direct influence denied to wealth, intellect, rank, or moral worth is more than compensated for by the indirect influence of their possessors over the general mass of voters: the wider the franchise, the more accurately does the elected Chamber represent the really operative factors in the nation. A democratic Parliament is thus far from representing nothing but the force of numbers.

To such arguments, as directed to the conditions that now prevail, there is one insuperable objection. They apply only to a state of things in which votes are given on grounds of principle, not at all to one in which elections turn on the private interests of individual voters. Yet in Great Britain, at the present day, interests are steadily superseding principles as the dominant note in politics. Many factors contribute to this undesirable result, but two of these are specially conspicuous: (i.) the intervention into politics of labour as an organised force, and (ii.) the growing tendency to invite voters to decide on particular, instead of general issues.

(i.) Great and increasing masses of voters are trade unionists in the first place, and Liberals or Conservatives only in the second. The Labour Party exists, not to further the welfare of the nation, but to help wage-earners at the expense of their employers and of the rest of the community. This conflict of interests is of obvious importance, at a time when fear to be outvoted by the other party prevents Liberals and Conservatives alike from giving whole-hearted opposition to trade-union demands, however unwarranted or inexpedient. The policy of these associations is not determined by the most capable artisans, but by the massed votes of workers of average or inferior skill. Parliament, when it bows to their authority, far from representing all classes in the nation, is not even representative of the best class of artisans.

The man who casts his vote as a member of a union—as a dock labourer, moulder, or engineer—rather than as a citizen of a great empire, affords one out of many examples of the tendency already noted to substitute interests for principles as the motive for political action. In this respect, a momentous change has been effected in the last fifty or even twenty-five years. During the greater part of the nineteenth century, the electors voted for principles or for party leaders, rather than for individual measures. So long as the electors grouped themselves according to broad issues of principle, their inherent sense of justice and fair play was likely to prevail: now that constant appeal is made to individual pockets, votes are governed by selfish interests.

(ii.) Modern doctrines like the "mandate" and modern devices like the Referendum, aiming at disentangling particular issues and submitting them one by one for the electors' approval, tend further to increase this danger. If, for example, the income-tax payer is directly asked whether he will pay one or two shillings in the pound, he could hardly be so neglectful of his wife and children (or for that matter of himself) as to vote for the higher rate. On the other hand, all who are subject only to indirect taxation and find their own burdens lightened by the increased income tax paid by others would combine to compel its progressive increase. A society reduced to its constituent atoms, deciding upon isolated issues, will be guided by appetite, not by reason. Masses, voting on this system, represent nothing higher than the gratification of purely physical wants. This is the only aspect in which men are really equal. Under a condition of society in which men vote on separate questions as each affects himself, the immediate gratification of the individual craving will outweigh all consideration for the well-being of the nation. Politics, thus conducted, is becoming a game of interests, in which principles count for little.

Modern conditions would thus seem to emphasise and stereotype the monopoly of power claimed by majorities. Both of the influences discussed, the action of trade unions and the practice of laying single issues before the electors, contribute to the triumph of numbers pure and simple. The increasing prominence of these two features in modern politics, effectually prevents the varied factors in the national life from obtaining even indirectly the influence which they should exert. The Parliament of the twentieth century no longer reproduces the varied aspects of English life as the Parliament of the fourteenth or even of the nineteenth century did. The Representative Chamber is to-day representative only of numerical majorities.

III. *Representation as a Condition precedent to Taxation.*

This doctrine has been adopted as a watchword by the friends of liberty and progress all the world over; but England claims to be its birthplace and its cradle. It was within the grey walls of the Chapter House at Westminster that this great principle of the modern world of politics was first applied to the problems of the Central Government. The medieval Parliament of the three estates, representing the three great classes of the realm, came into existence as a means of adjusting the incidence of the burden of taxation. To Edward I. and his Plantagenet successors, the presence of town and county representatives in their councils was required mainly, if not exclusively, to increase the efficiency of Parliament as a machine for raising money. In the centuries that followed, the House of Commons slowly tightened its grasp upon the national finance, until no tax could be initiated elsewhere. The chief function performed by the Representative Chamber in the middle ages was to prevent the Executive Government from making demands on the pockets of burgess or county freeholder without their own consent. Taxation and representation thus came to be inseparable. That doctrine, indeed, has been the germ and essence of the English Constitution throughout all stages of its growth and maturity. The great battles of English freedom have been won through the Chamber of the taxpayers gaining and keeping control over the purse-strings. "No taxation without representation" has been the underlying principle on which the foundations of constitutional liberty in the mother country and in all her self-governing dependencies have been laid. It has been borrowed from England by all foreign nations that have advanced on the road to political freedom. "No taxation without representation" was the battle-cry on which the American colonies waged their War of Independence. It was the plea with which they gained the sympathy of Chatham and of nearly half the British nation, and without which a mere appeal to brute force would never have been successful. It was thereafter adopted as the main pillar on which the Constitution of the United States was built.

Further illustrations are unnecessary. "No taxation without representation" has been adopted as an essential part of the polity of every nation or colony in every part of the civilised globe where free institutions have taken root. No one need wonder at the enthusiasm with which it has been acclaimed; for it is merely a translation into the sober language of political science of the popular adage that "he who pays the piper ought to call the tune." The best, and indeed the only, safeguard against the extravagance of an Executive Government, ever ready to further its own purposes with money taken from the people's pockets, is to require for every penny of taxation the consent of a Parliament that is truly representative of every class of those who have to pay.

Economists are unanimous in the opinion that this is the only sound basis of national finance. No body of men, however wise and honourable, can be trusted with unlimited powers of spending other people's money. If the tax-payers lose control of the taxing-machine, economy must sooner or later yield to extravagance; while all future interests will be sacrificed to the clamant needs of the present. Economists thus agree with constitutional theorists in their insistence on the doctrine that representation must never be divorced from taxation; and history supports them. The mutual dependence of the two things is the corner-stone of the British Constitution. Representative government has been identified in the past with a system that vested control over the Executive in a chamber composed of the tax-payers' representatives.

Of late years, both the theory and the practice of taxation have been silently and completely changed. The House of Commons, while making good in fact and law its claim to legislative omnipotence, has suffered essential alteration in its character. It is composed no longer of men chosen by the tax-payers, but rather of men appointed by those who expect to get rather than to give. It represents pensioners, or would-be pensioners, on the national bounties. The real tax-payers are the outvoted minorities who are unrepresented as such in the House of Commons. National finance is no longer controlled by those who pay, but by those who receive. Parliament acts no longer as a restraint upon the extravagance of the Executive or as a safeguard of the tax-payer's rights. It has become a stimulus to fresh expenditure; for each Member demands increased doles for the needy classes of his own constituency. It is the minority who pay and the majority who receive; and, as the effective part of Parliament is elected by this majority, it follows that representative government, in its ordinary and historical meaning, no longer exists in England. The rule that taxation and representation must go hand in hand has ceased to exist—has, indeed, been reversed completely.

This change, which undermines the very foundations of the British Constitution as laid by the Whigs in 1689, and accepted for two centuries by Conservatives, Liberals, and Radicals, has been effected by almost imperceptible degrees. So much so, that it is doubtful whether it has been generally realised even yet that the British Constitution as known to Conservatives like Blackstone and Disraeli, and to Liberals like Bentham, Hallam, and Macaulay has utterly ceased to exist. The old catchwords about taxation and representation are still in constant use; and few, apparently, who use them are aware that no corresponding reality now exists in British institutions.

The House of Commons, whose powers are, since 1911, practically synonymous with the powers of Parliament as a whole, now stands for a principle absolutely antagonistic to that of "No taxation without representation." The effective majority is able to reckon without its host. The issue of a general election turns on the wishes of those who, in the various forms of free education, old age pensions, State-aided insurance, or grants in aid, receive, directly or indirectly, more than they pay. Voters, desirous of obtaining for themselves or their dependants increased subsidies from the common purse, are invited by rival candidates to vote for their only true friend, the party which will guarantee the more lavish expenditure.

Democracy has, almost unperceived, made a gigantic advance upon the old doctrine which vested control over expenditure in representatives of those who had to pay. The profound nature of the change is intensified by two equally modern tendencies, the extension of the financial functions of the modern state, and the changed attitude towards the rights of private property. Each of these requires separate consideration.

IV. *The Proper Sphere of Parliamentary Finance.*

Very gradually at first, but with extreme velocity in the last decade, the sphere of taxation has expanded. The history of taxation in England, from the Norman Conquest to the present day, has been one of continuous growth. Whenever the revenue derived by the early kings from the royal estates and other sources was insufficient for the charges incident to the work of government, these kings through Parliament levied contributions upon the property of their subjects. The duties of the Executive were, however, strictly limited and defined by customary usage. The King enforced order, superintended the administration of justice, and acted as head of the national army. The objects for which contributions from private property could be demanded were thus few in number. They remained comparatively few even to the middle of the nineteenth century; for the influence of the favourite Liberal doctrine of *laissez faire* long restrained the Government and the Legislature from any avoidable interference with individual liberty and initiative.

That doctrine is to-day entirely discredited. No first-rate politician on either side has a word to say for it. With a velocity that has increased in geometric ratio within the last fifty, twenty-five, and ten years, the province alike of executive activity and of legislative interference with rights of liberty and property has been extended. Parliament and Cabinet by no means restrict themselves to managing the corporate business of the nation. The private affairs of every individual citizen and the defining of his relations with his neighbours have been brought within the sphere of government's action. The King's Ministers consider their most urgent duty to lie in readjusting, according to their own views of justice and social well-being, the balance between rich and poor.

Under the conditions that now prevail, the Ministry of the hour has full powers to put its theories rapidly into practice. Backed by a sufficient parliamentary majority, a modern Cabinet may force through its legislative programme without let or hindrance. Ministers have now no rivals to oppose their conscientious desire to redistribute the national dividend according to their own estimate of the wants and deserts of the voters on whose support they depend.

These are tremendous powers for an earthly omnipotence to exercise; and national weal or woe will depend on the spirit in which successive Cabinets approach their stupendous task. If those in power strenuously oppose all dangerous demands of their expectant beneficiaries; if they take no unnecessary risks and satisfy themselves by all reasonable precautions that their distributions of other people's wealth are so arranged as to do less harm than good; if they are sympathetic and scrupulously fair in adjusting the burden of taxation, and avoid the infliction of unnecessary hardships on numerically insignificant sections of the community; if they allow freedom of debate and full opportunities for the most unpopular classes to explain their objections to proposed confiscation of their goods; if they show solicitous care not to inflict even the semblance of a wrong on any trade or interest; if they are duly impressed with a deep sense of the tremendous responsibilities they incur, it is not impossible that national prosperity may be furthered by their efforts.

If, however, they are guided rather by a desire to retain popular favour and the power it brings, than by a sense of abstract justice; if they sacrifice the future to the present and the unpopular few to the powerful many; if they rush through Parliament ill-digested and half-debated measures; if they use their powers—powers unrivalled in magnitude and effectiveness since political institutions were invented—for party ends—punishing their political opponents and rewarding their supporters—they will in a brief space relax the moral fibre of the nation, until corruption destroys the body politic.

Human nature being what it is, pessimists will be found to doubt whether any body of politicians—or, indeed, any body of men—could safely be entrusted with power so vast and of such momentous consequences. Assuming, however, that successive Cabinets would not succumb to the temptations so thickly strewn about their path, it is still necessary to inquire what theoretical justification can be urged for establishing a dictatorship so supreme, a dictatorship that seeks to substitute Acts of Parliament for natural laws. To justify the right of a Cabinet, resting on a Parliament controlled by Government Whips, to determine the precise share of his own wealth that each individual may keep for himself and the share he must bestow on the beneficiaries nominated by the leaders of the party in power, would be a formidable task. A few disconnected suggestions are all that can be attempted here.

The national income is not the product of individuals working in isolation, but of their joint efforts. So far, all theorists are agreed; but difference of opinion arises as to the best method of distributing this national dividend. Economists maintain that only one method is compatible with justice or with the ultimate well-being of the State: namely, to leave the distribution to the operation of the laws of supply and demand. To tamper with these would be as futile as an attempt to forbid the tide's advance. This is the doctrine of the dismal science that the older schools of politicians were content to follow.

The doctrine of the new democracy is different. The King's Ministers, it is now maintained, through the docile instrumentality of a well-regulated Parliament, ought boldly to ignore the action of these natural laws, and distribute the national wealth, according to their own conception of abstract equity, among the various claimants who are their political friends and foes.

The full proof of the possibility of effecting such an artificial redistribution, without fatally diminishing the production of wealth, may be left to thoughtful reformers who have leisure to construct a new system of political economy, resting on principles not yet fully discovered. The justice and expediency of such a system are themes worthy of fuller discussion than they have yet received. However Liberals and Socialists may differ in discussing the theories that underlie recent expansions of the sphere of taxation, there is no doubt about the fact: Parliament now performs financial functions undreamt of twenty years ago.

V. *The Inviolability of Private Property.*

The new conception of the proper sphere and purpose of taxation has its counterpart in a revised estimate of the rights of private property. Leaders of thought in the last generation were unanimous in their belief that the inviolability of private property was an essential condition alike of security and of economic progress, which could not be disturbed without ultimate injury to poor as well as rich.

From Burke to Bentham, Conservatives and

Radicals were agreed that the welfare of the people and of posterity depended upon the strict observance of the boundary line between *meum* and *tuum.* The dividing wall, it was usual to consider, had been so built into the fabric of the national prosperity that it could not be removed without endangering the very foundations of order and progress. There have been times, indeed, in which tenderness for the assumed sanctity of property has been carried much too far. So much will readily be granted by many of those who fear that the danger now threatens from the opposite extreme.

If the claims of property are now to be supported at all, it can only be on the ground of utility to the State, not of any inherent sanctity of its own. The adamantine walls, indeed, that once separated *meum* and *tuum*, are now thin and yielding. Their power of resistance exists only on the sufferance of a thoroughly unsympathetic parliamentary majority. Vested interests of unpopular minorities in inherited wealth or even in the "unearned" income accruing on their invested savings have now no protection from the demands of a Parliament representing the classes to whom the old-fashioned virtue of thrift makes no appeal. The accumulated savings of past years lie at the disposal of a philanthropic Parliament, with ever-ready ear for the cries of the distressed who, perhaps through no fault of their own, have been unable to provide for themselves. In this way much old capital is reconverted into revenue and got rid of, the stimulus to accumulate new capital is weakened, and the survival and increased rate of propagation of the unfit are ensured.

In acting as a terrestrial providence, the Cabinet in power for the time being, when satisfied of the entire wisdom and justice of any proposed dislocation of economic conditions, has no obstacle to overcome in carrying out its benevolent purposes. The all-powerful Commons will vote to order along party lines without insisting on inconvenient amendments, and even without discussion, if the Government so desire.

The national Exchequer is one vast reservoir into which all forms of corporate or private wealth may be made to flow by use of the mechanical procedure for passing a Finance Bill into law. A Chancellor of the Exchequer, possessed of the confidence of his colleagues and with an effective following of grateful voters, recipients of past and future favours, can regulate the inflow of the resources of an empire, by simply pressing the button that completes the circuit: the sluice gates, as if worked by electricity, will obey his commands.

No such plenitude of power has ever before been enjoyed by any autocrat or dictator in any nation, ancient or modern, as is possessed under present democratic conditions in wealthy England by a Chancellor of the Exchequer, whose popularity makes him an indispensable member of a Cabinet. He may, by an obscure clause in a Finance Bill, so alter the conditions of trade and commerce as to make and mar the fortunes of thousands. He has full control over the increasing millions that every year flow through the Treasury on their journey from the pockets of one section of the electors into the pockets of another. This position of trust and power is one that even a god might envy, if sufficiently sure of his own omniscience not to be crushed under the burden of responsibility.

These new principles of finance (that property exists only on sufferance of Parliament, and that upon Parliament lies the duty of supplying out of the common purse the needs of all who have failed to help themselves) give peculiar poignancy to the divorce, previously unknown in the history of parliamentary government, between taxation and representation. The newer doctrines open wide and inviting vistas for large-hearted framers of modern Utopias; but it should not be forgotten that their realisation involves a complete reversal of fundamental principles once deemed essential in every constitutional State.

VI. *The Correspondence between Supply and Redress.*

No principle has contributed more to the building-up of English constitutional liberty than that which Hallam enthusiastically described as the mainspring of our Constitution, "that redress of grievances ought to have precedence of the grant of supplies." To illustrate Hallam's meaning in a manner adequate to the importance of the theme would involve the writing of six centuries of English history. That is unnecessary; for the connection between supply and redress is a commonplace of all writers on history and politics.

Parliament, throughout its struggle with the Executive, from the days of Edward I. to those of William III., always insisted on the necessity of the correspondence between supply and the redress of grievances. By this principle, an efficient check was placed on the exercise of arbitrary authority, and innumerable victories were gained for popular liberties. The efficacy of the remedy depended, however, on the division of functions. The supreme power lay with the Crown, but Parliament controlled the Crown through its control of the national purse. From Henry III. to Charles I., many an English king learned by bitter experience the meaning of the demand that discussion of grievances must have precedence over grant of supplies.

Under the modern democratic Constitution, this safeguard has ceased to act. The machinery that once checked despotic power is now at the despot's disposal. The Cabinet, having absorbed the royal prerogatives, has at the same time gained complete control over the taxing powers of Parliament; for a well-drilled House of Commons, reluctant to exchange the certitude of influence and salary for the chances of a general election, grants mechanically whatever tax the Cabinet decrees. It is no longer possible for the victims of tyranny to protect themselves by the withholding of supplies; while even the discussion of their grievances may be cut short by the ruthless closuring of inconvenient debates.[1] The time-honoured principle, correspondence between supply and redress, is no longer a safeguard against the abuse of power.

[1] Mr Asquith described closure by compartments as an attempt "to stifle the voice and paralyse the action of the House of Commons," and blamed it for hastening the day when that House would come to be "regarded as a mere automatic machine for registering the edict of a transient majority."—*Parl. Deb.*, 4th Series, vol. cxxxvii., p. 338 (1st July 1904).

VII. *The Doctrine of Checks and Balances.*

In one form or another, every well-ordered State must maintain a system of checks and balances as a bulwark between the citizen's rights and the arbitrary power of government. England, since the first beginnings of her political freedom, has had pre-eminently a balanced or mixed Constitution, in which the mutual interplay of different principles has prevented any one of them from usurping supreme power.

In estimating how far these checks and balances still safeguard individual rights, it is necessary to bear in mind the historical circumstances from which they arose. The King's caprice was the tyrant against which the first battles of English freedom were won. The Legislature acted as the much-needed check on the Executive. In the late Professor Seeley's phrase, the King was the governing organ: Parliament, the government-controlling organ. The original system of checks and balances was thus devised to protect popular rights against the monarch—to protect the many against the tyranny of one.

The present-day menace to liberty comes from a different quarter. Parliament, not the King, is now supreme. Individual rights are no longer invaded by arbitrary acts of Ministers in breach of law, but by the laws themselves—by statutes that override the rights of minorities in the interests of their political opponents. Power is no longer split up among various organs, enforcing mutual restraint. All fragments of authority, on the contrary, have now been collected together and placed under one guiding hand. There is only one tyrant whose caprice need now be dreaded, though this tyrant may, indeed, be variously described, either as the Cabinet controlling the legislative omnipotence of Parliament, or as Parliament carrying out the Cabinet's commands. Under either description, the essence of the matter is that the party leaders, between two general elections, are supreme, and may carry out their will in legislation and administration without dread of effective opposition. With the transference of supreme power from the King to the Ministers forced upon him by a parliamentary majority, the ancient system of checks and balances has ceased to act. The government-controlling organ has become the governing organ; and no new machinery has been devised to control the new despot who has thus usurped the throne.

Individual rights, whether of the nature of life, liberty, property, honour, or ambition, lie naked before the dissecting knife of legislative authority. Nothing stands between the subject and the ever-increasing demands of a Government that rests on a compact majority. The traditional safeguards of constitutional rights have now fallen to pieces. The individual is no longer protected by the distribution of powers between Legislature and Executive. The will of the Cabinet and the will of the omnipotent Parliament are now identical; and there is no power to which the wronged individual can appeal from their joint decision. The law courts afford no protection; for the party leaders whose will is the will alike of Cabinet and of House of Commons, do not scruple to introduce new legislation to overturn legal decisions of which their supporters disapprove. What has been done in the Taff Vale case will be done again in the case of Mr Osborne.

In a state of society in which supreme legislative and supreme administrative power are in league against the rights of minorities, it is the more necessary that the making of new laws should not be too rapid. This consideration leads to the discussion of another of the traditional checks and balances. It is a commonplace of text-books on the "mixed constitution" of Great Britain, that all classes are safe from the unjust encroachments of the Legislature, because no bill can reach the Statute Book without concurrence of King, Lords, and Commons.

If this safeguard of minorities was required

in the days when Legislature and Executive were normally opposed to each other, it is doubly necessary to-day. Yet it was only yesterday that it was finally destroyed. It is the boast of the Parliament Act of 1911 that the share of authority formerly possessed by the House of Lords has been reduced to impotence; while the shares once enjoyed by the King and the House of Commons respectively, have already been absorbed by the Cabinet. The balanced constitutional system of the Great Britain of an earlier day would thus seem, in all the characteristics once deemed essential, to have passed away.

Compared with the American Commonwealth, where an elaborate system of checks and balances continues in as full working order as when they were first devised in 1789, England at the present day is a far more thorough-going democracy. The Constitution of the United States was carefully framed to protect progressive minorities and the initiative of individual enterprise from the deadweight of majority pressure. It knows nothing of any doctrine like the sovereignty of Parliament, under which an ordinary legislative act has power to modify or annihilate the most cherished rights, or to authorise the repudiation of contractual obligations. Five barriers, on the contrary, protect the individual liberties of the American citizen:

the written Constitution which guarantees certain rights as fundamental: the distribution of authority between Congress and a President trammelled by no theories of ministerial responsibility: the division of power between federal and local state organs: the limited nature of the legislative authority enjoyed by Congress as a whole: and the co-ordinate rights vested in a Senate strongly rooted in popular affection, and therefore bold in using its powers against the will of the representative assembly. The democracy of Great Britain, now coming to its own, is free from all such shackles.

In England there is no written Constitution: no limits are placed to the scope of legislative activity in altering fundamental principles or attacking individual rights; the Executive is not independent of, but necessarily in close alliance with the Legislature: there are no separate organs of local government to balance the tremendous power wielded by the organs of the Central Government; while the House of Lords, as compared with the American Senate, is not only discredited in public estimation but is possessed of insignificant powers. In England, power has been focussed to one point. The once carefully divided legislative sovereignty has been collected in the hands of a House of Commons, representing nothing but numbers, and compelled by modern conditions to vote to the Cabinet's orders under closure and therefore without adequate debate. The doctrine of checks and balances, once reckoned an essential of our national well-being, is now a thing of the past.

This brief account of the gradual obliteration of ancient constitutional landmarks makes it obvious that the differences between our system of government as it stood in earlier ages and as it stands to-day are numerous and fundamental. When all the necessary subtractions have been made, but little of the time-honoured English Constitution remains. The alterations may, perhaps, be reduced to this, that a qualified or limited democracy has given place to an absolute one. The change may carry with it for the optimistic reformer the promise of untold blessings for the toiling millions of the future. Even those most ready to believe that Acts of Parliament are capable of creating a new heaven and a new earth will do well, however, to ask themselves how far it is wise to sacrifice, for a problematical gain, the principles that have made constitutional progress possible in the past.

CHAPTER II

THE CONSTITUTION OF TO-DAY COMPARED WITH THE CONSTITUTION OF FIFTY YEARS AGO

WALTER BAGEHOT'S *English Constitution*, written in 1868, still holds the field as the classic exposition of our modern system of government. Students who turn to his entrancing pages for guidance, need the emphatic warning that sweeping changes have been effected in the intervening period, both by legislation and by the rapid movement of opinion along democratic grooves. Before any attempt is made to indicate the more important divergencies between the Constitution of Lord Palmerston's day and that of our own, it may be well to examine briefly the features that Bagehot thought right to emphasise as most essential.

I. *Characteristics of the Mid-Victorian Constitution.*

To Bagehot, viewing the system actually at work in the years 1865 and 1866, and reviewing it again in 1872 in the valuable introduction to his second edition, published after the Reform Act of 1867 had been some years in operation, the outstanding characteristics were mainly five.

(1) *Cabinet Government.*—To begin with, he laid stress on what was then insufficiently appreciated but is now (thanks chiefly to his own elucidation) a commonplace of political thought, namely, the peculiar function performed by the Cabinet in producing harmony between the Legislature and the Executive. The entire working of the modern Constitution, he pointed out, depended on the central position of the British Cabinet, which was the pivot round which the whole machinery revolved. England, under the forms of a limited monarchy, had developed, almost without knowing it, a new type of polity, of which the essence was Cabinet government.

Queen Victoria, though titular Sovereign, could perform no single act of prerogative except through the agency of a Minister of the Crown, whose real title to office was the continued possession of the confidence of that House of Commons on which Her Majesty depended for necessary supplies; the chief among these Ministers were united in a Cabinet, whose members accepted full joint responsibility for every act performed by any one of them in pursuance of the common policy on which they had together taken office; and this Cabinet, under guidance of the Prime Minister as the admitted party chief, acted as a shield between the Monarch and liability, legal or political, for all acts of Government done in her name. This Cabinet acknowledged its responsibility to and dependence on Parliament, which was accepted as the only source of its political authority. A vote of no-confidence in the Ministry would be immediately followed by resignation. Cabinet and Parliament were necessarily in harmony. According as one side or the other of their complementary functions was emphasised, the whole system was designated either Cabinet government or Parliamentary government, which are accordingly two names for one institution.

Bagehot gave full weight to both aspects of the system: to its peculiar function of promoting the smooth working of our institutions by assuring for the Executive Government the permanent support of a sympathetic legislature, and to the manner in which it made good in practice the theoretical supremacy of the Legislature over the Executive. The first of these aspects of Cabinet government has at the present day suffered no alteration, but the second has been fundamentally modified. The Cabinet system still secures harmony between the King's Ministers and the House of Commons, but it no longer secures the subservience of the former to the latter. Since the Reform Acts of 1867 and 1884, the Cabinet and the constituencies have drawn closer together: the Lower House of Parliament has become less essential as a connecting link. A Cabinet that feels the people behind it is able to tyrannise systematically over its supporters in the Commons, to whom a general election would mean fresh expenses with possible loss of place and salary. Recent changes in parliamentary procedure also (necessary as these may possibly have been to enable an overburdened House to get through the increasing duties thrust upon it) have placed the Lower House more unreservedly in the hands of the party leaders.

It is true that in 1912 as in 1867 the same individuals who control the policy of the Cabinet are also the acknowledged leaders of the Commons: but in the interval a penetrating though subtle change has taken place. At present the Cabinet dominates Parliament, whereas in Bagehot's day Parliament dominated the Cabinet. Now as then, however, it is equally true that the Cabinet forms the central link in the system of government. Its essential feature is the responsibility of Ministers to the House of Commons and to the constituencies, as opposed to the American presidential system under which the executive head of the State owns no responsibility to the Legislature. President and Congress are co-ordinate and mutually independent authorities, each of which has its own exclusive province into which the other dare not intrude.

(2) *The Distinction between the Dignified and the Efficient Parts of the Constitution.*—A distinct but closely allied feature of the older Constitution, which Bagehot equally emphasised, was its division into two parts, which he called respectively its dignified and its efficient sides. The Crown, with its glamour of pomp and antiquity and its power of attracting the people's devotion, stood at the head of the august side of our institutions; the Prime Minister and his Cabinet, representing what was modern and utilitarian, stood at the head of the efficient side. In this connection, Bagehot was led to discuss, with a wealth of apposite illustration, the relations between the Monarch and the Ministers of the Crown, and such kindred topics as the extent and utility of the powers still actually left to the Sovereign's personal discretion.

This part of the discussion, interesting and important as it is, need not be dwelt upon, since no portion of Bagehot's work is better known. From his day until the close of King Edward's reign, no change in essentials had taken place in this respect. If that reign shows in some directions an increase in the personal influence of a popular Monarch, it shows in others some decline. At the date of King Edward's death, not only had the distinction between the august and the utilitarian sides of the Constitution remained unimpaired, but the balance between the two had not, perhaps, been materially altered. Of the momentous change effected since his death, it will be necessary to speak in the proper place.

(3) *Party Government.*—A third outstanding feature of the British Constitution as it mirrored itself in the mind of Walter Bagehot remains equally conspicuous and practically unchanged to-day. Party government is the system under which (unlike the group system of most continental states) the nation is divided for practical purposes into two great parties (or two fairly permanent coalitions of parties—which for practical purposes comes to the same thing), each of which is supreme by turns over the whole machinery of the State, executive and legislative. Party government, as thus defined, is as much an essential of our Constitution to-day, as it was in the middle of last century. The polity which, as we have seen, may indifferently be called either Parliamentary government or Cabinet government does not logically imply party government; but party government seems to be a condition of its highest level of success as a working system, and has been a marked feature

of the British polity since representative institutions were established.

Now as then, when a change of Ministers occurs, it occurs simultaneously all along the line. All portfolios are resigned at once. The entire Cabinet is reconstituted. The monopoly of power passes in a moment from one party to their opponents. Further, as the change in the complexion of the Ministry is necessarily due to a change in the complexion of the Commons' majority, the same party that triumphs in the Legislature must also triumph in the Executive. Party government implies that the same party which rules the dominant House of Parliament must have exclusive entry to the Cabinet, and controls the policy of every department of the Imperial Government. As all this remains unaltered, it is unnecessary to discuss the penetrating analysis given by Bagehot of the merits of the system, or of its dangers and their antidotes. The passage is well known to students of English institutions.[1]

(4) *The Supremacy of the House of Commons.*—Upon no aspect of the Constitution was Bagehot more emphatic than on the dominating position occupied by the House of Commons in deciding all questions of national policy, whether domestic or foreign, legislative or administrative. "The ultimate authority,"[2] he declares, "in the English

[1] Pages 176-194 (ed. of 1904). [2] Page 227.

Constitution is a newly elected House of Commons." No matter what may be the nature of the problem requiring attention, "a new House of Commons can despotically and finally resolve." It is this feature that gives to our system a unity, simplicity, and effectiveness, in his opinion, in contrast with composite governments like that of the United States, "in which the supreme power is divided between many bodies and functions." He holds the excellence of the British Constitution to be "that it has achieved this unity."[1] Bagehot is, however, careful to qualify these statements by pointing out that its success "could not have been thoroughly achieved except for two parts, which I venture to call the 'safety-valve' of the Constitution, and the 'regulator.'"[2] The "safety-valve," which is now of comparatively slight importance, he describes as the means whereby "the head of the Executive can overcome the resistance of the Second Chamber by choosing new members of that Chamber"; this is the so-called power of "swamping the Lords."

What Bagehot terms the "regulator" is more important to the present argument. The regulator, as he tells us, "of our single sovereignty" (that is the necessary machinery for controlling in case of necessity the otherwise dictatorial power of the House of Commons

[1] Page 229. [2] Page 229.

of his own day) is the Crown's prerogative of dissolving Parliament. To the chief executive there is confided "the power of dissolving the otherwise sovereign Chamber."[1] In expounding the importance of this "regulator," Bagehot not merely admits, but emphasises an element of danger inherent in the system he has been praising. If Constitutions under which all real power is focussed to one point are the most efficient, they are also most dangerous to individual liberty. The distribution of power may weaken the organs of Government in the execution of their proper functions, but it weakens also their power of encroaching on the rights of others. Bagehot, if he had witnessed the developments of recent years, might have dwelt more than he did on this aspect. As it was, he made clear his conviction that there must be a check to incipient despotism somewhere. The danger that the Commons, in whom in his day the supreme power was vested, would abuse that power was provided against by the operation of the Crown's prerogative of dissolution. The Executive had power to dissolve the Lower House whenever it threatened to give full rein to the spirit of caprice and injustice which, in his opinion, is inseparable from the enjoyment of unbridled powers.[2]

[1] Page 230. [2] Pages 230-231.

In all this, he was treating (as, in the conditions prevailing in his own day, he was bound to do) the House of Commons as an independent organ acting habitually on its own initiative, and not merely as an automaton for registering the Cabinet's decrees. The Commons at that date had by no means handed over their own great powers to the control of the Cabinet. It was the House of Commons which (save for this "regulator") would have completely dominated the Cabinet; and thus the prerogative of dissolution supplied the needed check on the swollen ambitions of the only organ then strong enough to threaten the equilibrium of the State.

Now, it is the Cabinet that permanently dominates the Commons, and therefore it is against the Cabinet's tendencies to dictatorship that a "regulator" is needed. Bagehot's check on incipient despotism is no longer effective. The "prerogative" that could extinguish at a moment's notice the despot of the Palmerstonian Constitution, has now gone to swell the already excessive authority of the despot of to-day. Both sets of powers are concentrated in one hand. From one general election to another, there is no machinery in operation to turn a Cabinet out of office, however it may abuse its trust. The "regulator" no longer acts.

(5) *The Distribution of Political Power.*—The

Palmerstonian Constitution, as Bagehot repeatedly reminds his readers, was by no means a pure democracy. Under it, on the contrary, power was monopolised by the middle and upper classes. It was a system under which the aristocracy and the plutocracy balanced each other, and divided all real power between them. This result was due partly to the restricted nature of the franchise; but even more to a sociological phenomenon of which Bagehot never tires of reminding his readers, a phenomenon which he was not without hope might continue in operation even after the extension of the franchise in 1867. This vital factor in the political life of his own day is discovered by Bagehot in a peculiar attitude of the lower classes towards the social superiors to whom they had been accustomed for centuries past to look for leadership. This he describes as the "deferential" frame of mind, and it furnishes the keynote to his whole account of the Palmerstonian Constitution as an actually working system.

This spirit of deference, indeed, he considered essential to the success and to the very existence of Cabinet or Parliamentary government, as known to him. "I have said that Cabinet government is possible in England because England was a deferential country. I meant that the nominal constituency was not the real constituency; that the mass of the 'ten-pound' householders did not really form their own opinions, and did not exact of their representatives an obedience to those opinions; that they were in fact guided in their judgment by the better educated classes; that they preferred representatives from those classes and gave those representatives much license."[1]

The mass of the old electors, he explains with his felicitous, light touch, "liked to have one of their 'betters' to represent them; if he was rich, they respected him much; and if he was a lord, they liked him the better. The issue put before these electors was which of two rich people will you choose? And each of those rich people was put forward by great parties whose notions were the notions of the rich—whose plans were their plans. The electors only selected one of two wealthy men to carry out the schemes of one of two wealthy associations."[2] It is difficult to realise that it was only forty years ago that these words were written: the "deferential" attitude of the British labourer or artisan to the so-called upper classes, is, for good or evil, a thing of the past.[3]

[1] Introduction, p. xii. [2] Page xiii.

[3] Mr Sidney Low, in his admirable sketch of the Constitution as it stood in 1904 (*Governance of England*, p. 176) still adheres to Bagehot's estimate of the deferential attitude of the masses. This opinion of an acute observer only shows the rapid march of events in the last eight years.

II. *Points of Contrast with Modern Constitution.*

Of the stupendous changes that have been wrought in the last forty years, some have been effected by statutes; some by the silent processes of growth and decay that are constantly at work in institutions as in men; some by the ebb and flow of public opinion and the psychological attitude of the minds that form it. Some are of the nature of alterations in the mechanism of government; some consist in the changed ideas of the scope and purport of legislation; and some of the most vital result from the utterly different temper that has come to prevail in current politics.

The most potent factor in the change has been the silent revolution gradually effected in the mental and moral atmosphere that envelops legislators and electors. To begin with, the characteristic on which Bagehot lays such stress, the "deferential" attitude of the labouring classes, which in his opinion made representative government possible, has completely disappeared. Electors are no longer content to select independent men of the better class and leave them to act as they think fit. This alone is sufficient to account for a complete change in the whole spirit of the Constitution; but it has been accompanied by crucial modifications of almost every important organ of government and of their relations to each other.

(1) *The Composition of the House of Commons.*—The People's Chamber has undergone vital alterations in its composition, while it has widely increased the range of its authority. Successive extensions of the franchise in 1867 and 1884 have altered the character of the House, Bagehot's description of which accordingly requires fundamental modification. It is no longer true to say with Bagehot that the Representative Chamber is too favourable to the landed interest, or too aristocratic in its composition, or that it totally fails to represent the important class of artisans. It would be absurd to say of it to-day that it is plutocratic rather than democratic in its outlook, or that it only represents the views of monied and aristocratic minorities.

(2) *Relations between Electorate and Commons.*—The "deferential" attitude of the multitude of voters had its natural complement in the great measure of independence enjoyed by their representatives in Parliament. In the last fifty years the electorate has increased the closeness of its supervision and the Commons have been reduced to servitude. The change began with the new influences introduced into politics with the Reform Act of 1867. Mr Francis Holland, in his admirable continuation of Erskine May's

Constitutional History, has given the best analysis yet published of these changes and of the reasons for them. Contrasting the effects of the Act of 1867 with those of the Act of 1832, he explains how "the first great extension of the suffrage made the electorate independent of the Crown; the next great extension was destined to bring the House of Commons under the control of the electorate."[1] The reasons are not far to seek. The extension of the franchise to the working-men of the towns in 1867 made it necessary for both parties to bestir themselves to catch the newly created votes. As humble suitors for election, candidates came to explain with ever-increasing fulness the details of their policy to the new classes of electors. Constrained more and more to bind themselves to satisfy specific demands, they lost their independence and sank to the level of mere delegates.

Before 1867 a House of Commons, once elected, enjoyed almost perfect freedom of action. The electors had no initiative in the making of laws. The party leaders made no prior announcements as to the policy they intended to carry out, should they be entrusted with power. The practice of "stumping the country" was practically unknown.[2] Since 1867, definite party programmes are placed before the electors, who demand specific pledges, sometimes on minute

[1] Page 18. [2] *Ibid.*, p. 19.

points of details and on matters directly affecting their own class interests. Members of Parliament find themselves entangled in a complete network of promises and understandings, which prevent them from using their own judgment as to what is best for the nation whose laws they make.

(3) *Relations between Commons and Cabinet.*—The Act of 1867, which subjected the Commons to the electorate, has also subjected them to the authority of the Cabinet. The leading Ministers, finding that the only road to power is to address mass assemblages in various parts of the country, and to obtain the voters' confidence by meeting them face to face, now look rather to the electors than to the Commons as the power that keeps them in office. Legislative control and initiative have thus been transferred from the House of Commons, partly to the people themselves and partly to the Cabinet "through the opening as it were," so Mr Holland suggestively expresses it, "of direct communication between the Cabinet and the country."

This is the foundation of that ascendency which a modern Cabinet exercises over the House of Commons in marked contrast to the relations between these two organs of the Central Government as they presented themselves to Bagehot. The shifting of the centre of sovereignty has been accelerated by improvements in party organisation and in parliamentary procedure, among which it is only necessary to mention the increased authority of party Whips, the encroachments on the time allotted to private members and consequent monopoly of legislative initiative by the Government, and the cutting short of discussion by the drastic use of the closure.

If part of the ancient authority which the Lower House has lost has been directly gathered to themselves by the electors, another part has been added by the Cabinet to the excessive power it already enjoyed. There is now little possibility of a House of Commons turning against the Cabinet whose guidance it is accustomed to follow almost blindly. If one section of its majority seems restive, it can readily be lulled into quiescence again by judicious concession at the expense of the common enemy. Few members are so independent as to refuse reasonable terms of accommodation. They have no wish to lose their seats and salaries, and to incur at the same time a quarrel with the all-powerful party managers.

In normal circumstances, a Cabinet may safely count on a secure tenure of office from one general election to the next, unless for tactical reasons it decides on risking an earlier appeal to the country. For a period of five years, the electors are powerless against a Cabinet which has usurped all the executive powers placed by law in the hands of the King, and all the legislative powers placed in the hands of Parliament.[1]

(4) *The House of Lords.*—The Parliament Act of 1911, whether or not we regard it as mainly declaratory of accepted constitutional conventions, now regulates the relations between the Chambers. Sufficient time has not yet elapsed to furnish data for an exhaustive discussion of the consequences of that statute. Unlooked-for effects may be found lurking in its clauses. In the actual letter of the law, for instance, the Act would seem to have increased in one material respect the powers of the Upper Chamber.

The House of Lords, in its desire for peace, allowed (through many centuries of disuse) its once acknowledged right of amending money bills to fall into desuetude. As no statute was ever passed to define the extent of the powers thus lost, the House of Commons made consistent efforts to interpret the disability of the rival Chamber as broadly as possible; and the Lords were strategically too weak to resist. The Lower House claimed all doubtful bills as money bills; and showed a tendency, when any non-financial measure was frustrated by the Lords, to reincorporate its main provisions in

[1] *Cf.* Sidney Low, *Governance,* p. 81: "In our modern practice the Cabinet is scarcely ever turned out of office by Parliament *whatever it does.*"

the body of what they claimed to be a money bill. They thus defeated the Lords' right to amend, and made rejection difficult and dangerous. The Parliament Act, by providing machinery for distinguishing between money bills and ordinary bills, has restored to the Upper House the effective right to amend a large class of bills which the Commons previously claimed as unamendable. A statute thrust by the Commons upon an unwilling House of Lords, has thus confirmed the Lords' legal right freely to amend all bills declared by the Speaker not to be money bills. The House of Commons can hardly challenge the decision of their own Speaker, or the authority of rules of their own devising.

The possession of legal rights avails little, however, to a Chamber whose unpopularity prevents it from exercising any part of its acknowledged rights, without danger of evoking threats of punishment by the forcible intrusion into its membership of Government nominees to override the decisions of its legitimate members. If it is impossible to induce self-respecting gentlemen to accept peerages on such terms, constitutional law lays down no qualifications for the post; and doubtless a sufficient number of "cuckoo peers" of some sort could readily be obtained, pledged to justify their forced intrusion by performing the acts of destruction required of them. Briefly, then, the House of Lords which, in Bagehot's opinion, had not sufficient power to resist the maturely formed will of a determined House of Commons, has now less power than ever, and would be unwise to attempt resistance against the Cabinet's dictatorship.

The Parliament Act, it may be pointed out, has contributed towards changing the legislative conditions of the House of Commons as they prevailed in Bagehot's day. Any controversial measure advocated by a Government to which the Lords are opposed, must be introduced as early as possible in the life of a quinquennial Parliament. This means congestion in the first year of a newly elected House of Commons. It means also an unreality in the discussion of a measure which, it is known, will be certainly thrown out "in another place." Finally, when the measure, in the form of a third bill, enters at last the arena of practical politics, both its supporters and opponents, wearied by the sham discussions of two previous sessions, will be apt to rest content with a perfunctory recapitulation of arguments that have grown stale. Bills will be forced through, without substantial amendment, in the exact form in which they were originally introduced. The House of Lords will thus cease to perform the normal services of a real revising chamber. Its old function of forcing a compromise in the interests of defeated minorities will be henceforward impossible.

(5) *Relations between King and Cabinet.*—The present reign, young as it is, has already opened a new chapter in the relations between the Crown and its Ministers. On 16th November 1910, six months after King Edward's death, a momentous interview took place between King George and two representatives of the party in power. These representatives were the Prime Minister and the Leader of the Liberal Party in the House of Lords. It was the latter who made the fullest and final official report of what had taken place at the interview. The Marquess of Crewe, in the House of Lords on 8th August 1911, in performing what he admitted to be a painful task, disclosed, so far as the Government deemed expedient, the circumstances under which the Prime Minister had wrung from his Sovereign a reluctant consent to create, in a certain contingency that had not yet arisen, peers in sufficient number to force the Parliament Bill through the Upper Chamber.

Lord Crewe began by describing the policy of a wholesale creation of peers as a "lamentable necessity," but, later on, feeling these words to be inadequate, he proceeded to characterise it as an "odious business."[1] His lordship was appar-

[1] "The whole business, I frankly admit, is odious to me." —*Parl. Deb.*, ix., p. 342.

ently unable to suggest any precedents for the Prime Minister's action in forcing His Majesty to mortgage his future freedom of decision, by giving "contingent guarantees" as to the use to be made of the royal prerogative in certain problematical circumstances that might never have arisen. The incident, in truth, is entirely unprecedented. As Lord St Aldwyn in the course of the debate forcibly declared: "The action of the Government has deliberately placed him [King George] in the most cruel position any English Sovereign has been placed in for more than a century."[1]

Chief Justice Coke in 1616 was pressed by James I. to pledge himself in advance to decide, in the manner desired by the King, a case which was then pending. But he would give no other reply than this, that "whenever the case should come before him, he would do what was fitting for a judge to do."[2] King George's position was one of incalculably greater difficulty. If he had not been denied (unfairly denied, as many high authorities maintain) the opportunity of hearing the matter argued from the point of view of His Majesty's Opposition, he might, perhaps, have decided to adapt Coke's formula to his own

[1] Full details on the whole subject will be found in a powerful article contributed by Mr J. A. R. Marriott to the *Fortnightly Review* for September 1911.

[2] S. R. Gardiner, *Hist. of England*, iii., 19.

needs, declaring that when the problematical had become actual, he would then do what was fitting for a constitutional Monarch to do.

The analogy between the two cases is far from complete. The hazards incurred by Coke, in resisting the improper demands of his King, were light as compared with those that would be incurred by a constitutional Monarch who was so bold as to resist Ministers whom he could not do without. While loyal subjects of all parties had no feelings but those of profound sympathy for His Majesty, placed on the cruel horns of a dilemma, there seems little doubt of the impropriety of the action of the Government in forcing a still uncrowned sovereign, with no experience of the rights and duties of kingship, into a position at once equivocal and unparallelled, in pursuance of a policy described by its promoters as "lamentable" and "odious."

The incident is a disagreeable one, and Ministers who are jointly responsible for its occurrence are naturally anxious that it should be forgotten. But its effects in lowering the prestige, and diminishing the usefulness of constitutional Monarchy cannot be ignored. What the Crown has lost, the Cabinet has acquired. The modern efficient parts of the Constitution have gained a new triumph over the dignified, august parts.

(6) *Checks and Balances.*—Walter Bagehot,

in his anxiety to counteract the exaggerations of Blackstone, ran some danger of falling into exaggerations of his own, when he came near denying that the doctrines of "the distribution of powers" and of "checks and balances" had any place in the British Constitution of his day. So far from effective power being split up among monarchic, aristocratic, and democratic elements; among King, Lords, and Commons; or between those entrusted with legislative and administrative functions respectively, the supreme authority in England, he insisted, was focussed to one point, and centred in one supreme organ, namely, "a newly elected House of Commons."

There is truth, as well as force, in what he said; but he would seem here, in his eagerness to correct the misstatements of others, to have laid himself open to a danger of misconstruction in an opposite direction. In his bald statement, made with one particular purpose in view, he seems to have lost sight of some other not unimportant aspects. It may be pointed out, for example, that a House of Commons is not always newly elected and that in his day even more than in our own, a House of Commons, grown old and discredited, might be incapable of attempting any stretch of dictatorial power. Further, Bagehot himself has insisted on the important function played by the "regulator" of the whole constitution, namely, the power of the prerogative to force an appeal to the country by dissolving Parliament.

A more searching criticism may be hazarded of Bagehot's presentment of the problem. No doubt, as he rightly points out, the House of Commons by its alliance with the Cabinet and the electorate, and its consequent power to brush aside in the long run all opposition to its mature, determined, and persistent will, has *virtually* obtained control over all the other organs in the State. This, however, is a very different thing from the direct vesting by law of all power in one particular institution. The House of Commons dominated the situation only so long as its majority remained in harmony with the Executive Government, and only so long as that majority felt confident that it had the country at its back. Otherwise, it might have had its measures thrown out by the House of Lords, or it might have been dissolved against its will by the Cabinet.

The Cabinet system stands not for unqualified unity, but rather for unity in diversity; and to that extent embodies, while it modifies, the doctrine of "the distribution of powers." Legislative power forty years ago, except for the short period immediately following an election fought on a definite issue and in respect of that issue, was not absolutely monopolised by the Lower House. As matter of history, the House of Lords has dealt a death blow to many important measures since Bagehot wrote. "Checks and balances" undoubtedly existed in England in 1867; and that fact need not be denied because of the exaggerations made by Blackstone a hundred years earlier.

It is very different in 1912. These checks and balances have almost completely ceased to act, because of the changes of the last forty years. The process still continues: only last year, the Cabinet took another step towards the complete enslavement of the Crown, and then proceeded to mutilate the House of Lords; while the power of resistance or delay formerly enjoyed by minorities in the Commons has been neutralised by recent standing orders altering procedure drastically in favour of the driving power of the Government. However inadequate they may have been in Bagehot's day, checks and balances did exist; but they have now been brushed aside by a Cabinet intent on establishing its own dictatorship.

(7) *The Spirit of the Constitution.*—Great as have been the changes effected by statute and standing order, their effect has been intensified by changes in the attitude in which political problems are now approached. In particular, the startling extension of the sphere and frequency of legislation has altered the background of everything. The Government

now undertakes tasks which fifty years ago it would not have dared to attempt; it overrides rights of liberty and property in a way that would not have been tolerated by the men of the last generation. The emphatic manner in which the so-called "deferential" attitude of the working classes has been discarded, has already received sufficient notice.

Alterations in the spirit of the whole have thus contributed to the breakdown of constitutional safeguards, and to the consequent rightlessness of minorities. With all these elements of change, both in the framework of the Government and in the spirit in which it is worked, acting and reacting on each other, the great gulf that separates the Palmerstonian Constitution from that of the twentieth century becomes apparent.

CHAPTER III

TENDENCIES OF DEMOCRATIC LEGISLATION

MODERN Democracy with the optimistic buoyancy of youth, sets forth to remodel the world by means of legislation. Its guiding axioms, of whose truth it rests assured, are these: that nothing can be safely left to chance; that the conscious reason of the nation must modify or supersede the natural effects of the rules of supply and demand; that the State has the right to impose its absolute will (that is the will of a majority) on all classes and individuals; that a House of Commons, freely elected by the equal votes of the people, is the proper organ for expressing the will of the State; that no provision made by a statute passed by such a House can be reckoned an injustice; that it is possible under all circumstances, by means of statutory enactments, to further national prosperity, and, if not directly to increase the sum of human happiness, at least to "hinder human misery." The more of such enlightened legislation a nation has, the better and happier it ought to be.

No set of maxims could be more opposed to those under which Liberalism won its triumphs in the first half of the nineteenth century. In the creed of Bright and Cobden, of Bentham, the Mills, and of Herbert Spencer, the fewer statutes interfering with the natural laws of supply and demand, the better. This individualistic distrust of legislation was the first principle of the system of economics known to our fathers as "free-trade." For them, the legitimate work of Government was confined to three objects:—to maintain order, to enforce contracts, and to preserve a fair field for individual enterprise. The individual, so they thought, knew better what was good for him, and the best way to get it, than any organ of Government, however loud might be its claim to omniscience. The nation, they argued, was composed of individuals, and in the long run must suffer from every unnecessary restraint placed upon private initiative. Children might need protection: grown men were better left to stand on their own feet, than to be drilled by a paternal government to walk along lines prescribed.

The triumph of socialistic ideals over the traditional Liberal maxims has implied a sharp change of outlook. The individual citizen is no longer trusted to mould his own destiny.

His freedom, prospects in life, and property are surrendered to the philanthropic guidance of Government organs which, by legislative and administrative supervision, are ready to take better care of him than he can take of himself. This supervision, galling to the ambitious and progressive minority, will work (it is hoped) miracles for the masses with whom self-help is unpopular or impossible. An iron network of conditions, regulated by a mass of statutes which only men of leisure have time to read, has thus been woven round the freedom of the citizen, who can hardly move among the meshes of innumerable Acts of Parliament whose very titles be has barely heard.

The activity of the modern House of Commons, as an instrument of the sovereign people's will, recalls the activity of the old Star Chamber as an instrument of Tudor and Stewart kings. Of that august weapon of tyranny, it has been well said that nothing was too high to defy its attack, nothing too trivial to escape its scrutiny and control. The power of the modern Parliament, however, is more deeply rooted; and its action, with all the resources of modern science and civilisation at its command, a thousand times more penetrating and thorough. Legislation, as it were by the mere pressing of an electric button, can silently transform the whole face of society. There is another difference—and one which operates in favour of the modern engine of supreme power: while the Star Chamber often acted rather in the interests of the few than of the many, the House of Commons always acts in the name of the sovereign people. In practice, however, the will of the people is the will only of somewhat more than half of them. To the defeated half, subjection to the wishes of their more numerous opponents may not be less hateful than subjection to an autocrat, meting out stern justice to all and sundry. Oppression by the many, indeed, may be harder to bear than oppression by the few.

The powers, moreover, of the dreaded Star Chamber were trivial and insignificant compared with those of a modern House of Commons. It is notable that three separate movements should at the present day have converged to one goal:—The tendency of legislation to regulate the most intimate details of the subject's life has been combined with the claims of one House of Parliament to a monopoly of legislative power, and with the demand that that House should represent the brute voting power of numbers and nothing else. Each of the three movements seems now at the point of culmination. It will take some years, however, before the nature of the inevitable consequences can be fully realised.

I. *The Era of Legislative Action supersedes the Era of Free Contract.*

Great Britain, for good or evil, is entering on a new stage of her development. The nature of the change may be considered in the light of a phrase made famous by the late Sir Henry Sumner Maine, that "society progresses from status to contract." He meant that under early civilisation, as illustrated still by the hide-bound condition of some parts of the unchanging East, individuals, fettered by the rules of caste, live and die under conditions determined by the mere fact of birth, powerless to alter their lot according to their personal wishes; whereas, in advanced societies, a man determines his life and employment to a great extent by his own efforts and ambitions, regulating his lot in life by agreements into which he voluntarily enters. In this way, the era of status gradually gave place to the era of contract.

Maine's formula, regarded as a complete summary of human progress, is incomplete. It limits itself to two stages, where at least three exist. While the era of status, implying the individual's enslavement to caste and the accident of birth, gave way to the era of contract, where everything is determined by the conscious interplay of individual wills left free to adjust their destinies as they can or may; that era in turn is rapidly giving way to a third, in which legislation plays the leading rôle—where the conscious action of the will of the majority interferes with the individual's right to enforce contracts, and re-adjusts, according to its own conception of right and wrong, the conditions of life. Each man is no longer left to reap where he has sown. Far from it; statutes lay down what contracts may and what may not be entered into; what contracts may with impunity be broken; and what modifications in their terms and substance must be made by one of the contracting parties for the benefit of others. An era in which every man's life is regulated by Act of Parliament is now succeeding one in which it was determined by the play of free contract.

There would seem to be three stages in the progress of the world—status, contract, legislation. A fuller formula is thus required than that of Maine; and it may perhaps be embodied in some such words as these—"Society progresses from status to legislation through an intermediate stage of contract." This third stage is arriving more quickly and thoroughly in Britain than elsewhere, for the English Parliament, unlike the legislatures of other civilised and freedom-loving countries, has absolutely no restriction upon its unfettered discretion. In the newly dawning era, then, in which everything will depend on statutory regulation, in which all men will look to Parliament as the supreme arbiter of destinies as well as the restrainer of liberty and the distributor of property, it becomes of prime importance for every citizen, whether he has anything to lose or everything to gain, to form some conception of the probable trend of the legislation of the future. Is it possible to discover any tendencies that are likely to remain constant in shaping the endeavours of the 670 elected Members of Parliament who act as our terrestrial providence? The trend of modern legislation will require to be considered under several heads.

II. *Capital and Labour.*

The Imperial Parliament, following the bold example of the Australian legislature, is destined, sooner or later, to take into its own hands the settlement of those trade disputes which become every year more frequent, inflicting cruel suffering on thousands of men, women, and children, exhausting the resources of capital and the reserves of labour, and threatening irreparable damage to the economic well-being of England in its competition with foreign nations.

Startling results may be expected to follow the completion of the movement, already begun, for transferring the adjustment of the relations of capital and labour from the realm of contract (or collective bargaining) to that of direct legislation. The one merit that can be claimed for the existing method of settling disputes by conference and compromise, backed by the brutal expedients of lock-outs and strikes, is that it does not unduly favour either party to the dispute. Capital and labour both suffer severely, while the bone for which they fight may fall to foreign dogs; but ultimately something approximating to just relations is, for the time being, established between the combatants.

The steps leading to compromise are only too well known. In the normal case, a joint conference is held between a small number of representatives selected by the men and an equal number of delegates from the associations of their employers. The accredited agents of capital and labour meet face to face, and settle their differences, in accordance with economic laws of supply and demand, by discussion and mutual concession. The circumstances of such a meeting secure a fair field for both combatants, each of whom is free to wrest from the needs or timidity of the other, such terms as he can; while the Government avoids all arbitrary interference and restricts itself to its proper functions of preserving order, or gives, if requested, the services of the Board of Trade as an influential mediator.

When the Legislature comes to assume in England, as it has already done in Australia, the duty of settling labour disputes, all this will be changed. Labour, at present restricted to an equal voice with capital in the old arena of conference and private agreement, will enjoy an overwhelming superiority in the new arena of legislation. If labour votes solid, no one who opposes its claims, however exorbitant or however ruinous for future British trade these claims may be, can possibly obtain election to Parliament. One party to the dispute, then, will be certain of a compact body of votes in the House of Commons pledged to its support, and will be able to use these votes for the furtherance of its own ends.

No revolution will be needed to effect this radical alteration of existing conditions. This transference of the economic centre of the nation from the sphere of collective bargaining to that of legislative enactment is already being effected noiselessly and almost unobserved. No threats need be used; no bloodshed feared. The House of Commons has merely to exercise, by the ordinary course of legislation, the monopoly of power already conceded to it. There are now no legal or constitutional limits to its authority; no checks to overrule its decisions or seriously delay their execution. The masses of skilled and unskilled labourers, forming, it may well be, a majority of voters, have already the means in their own hands: they need not wait until the unequal balance is, by abolition of plural voting and by registration reforms, still further tilted in their favour. When the decisions of law courts or the results of conferences between masters and men fail to give complete satisfaction to the mass of employees, they have only to issue orders to their representatives in Parliament to alter the existing law, and the thing is done. A subservient legislature will readily reverse the findings of impartial judges and authorise the repudiation of bargains, if sufficient pressure is applied at the right time to rival candidates eagerly competing for election.

When the process of transference is complete, strikes and labour wars will be at an end; but only because of the complete triumph of one party to the struggle. In a tribunal appointed by the equal votes of individuals, how can a few hundreds or thousands of employers expect to obtain an equal number of representatives with the millions of their own employees? The masters' present power of self-protection will silently fall from them, with the silent extension of the normal sphere of parliamentary intervention. No opportunity will be afforded of even striking a blow in their own defence. If Parliament, pledged to befriend wage-earners, should be called upon to fix the minimum wage for any trade, after a conference has failed to bridge the gulf between the rate offered and the rate demanded, it cannot long hesitate to obey the mandate of the more numerous section of its constituents. Once a clear issue has been raised between 27s. and 30s. as a minimum wage, the decision is undoubted. The higher rate will prevail. There is no reason, however, why this figure should be long maintained. If progressive demands are made for 35s. and 40s., they must in due course be conceded. *À priori*, no maximum can be fixed.

At this point, economists may intervene to remind us of the fixed laws of supply and demand which not even King Demos with all his legislative omnipotence could dare to override; but unfortunately these fixed laws contain nothing to prevent an unwise attempt to set them for the moment at defiance. The catastrophe may be deferred but is inevitable. Grievous, perhaps irremediable, harm may have been done before the avengers of outraged nature act. The longer the floods are dammed back, the greater will be the havoc wrought by the final burst. In some cases, it is true, punishment may fall rather on the next generation than on that which commits the offence. Such considerations bring slender consolation to any one but the professional demagogue.

Theorists point out, with perfect truth, that

in the long run the interests of capital and labour are identical; that present injustice done to either will in time hurt both; and that it is to the ultimate benefit of all concerned, to adopt a scale of wages in accordance with the conditions that would naturally regulate a labour market undisturbed by legislative experiments.

All this is true; but such considerations are apt to be ignored by a People's Chamber under strong temptation to be influenced by the needs of the moment rather than by distant contingencies. "After us the deluge" is apt to be the unconscious motto that determines their policy. A Chamber that represents majorities cannot afford to hold the balance even between two forces with widely different voting powers. The dice are necessarily loaded against capital. The fact that the interests of non-union workers and of specially skilled union workers (to say nothing of the entire body of wage-earners in the future) are often identical with those of capitalists merely makes the consequences more far reaching.

Meanwhile, pending their own expected triumphs, the advocates of the rights of labour combine with telling effect two methods of gaining their ends. Pressure is exercised through the Representative Chamber in order to paralyse the action of the Executive in suppressing the disorderly and lawless practices that accompany strikes; while universal strikes are threatened as a means of compelling legislation with a bias in favour of labour. When "peaceful" picketing was declared illegal, a House of Commons subservient to the clamour of majorities quickly made it legal. If the Legislature hesitates to fix the minimum wage desired, a general strike supplies the needed stimulus. Peaceful parliamentary action and syndicalism, accompanied by acts of violence, move hand in hand. What force fails to accomplish, may safely be left to guile. Society in progressing from contract to legislation deals an immediate blow at capital; and in destroying capital it will ultimately injure labour too.

III. *Landlords and Tenants.*

The manner in which the future relations of capital and labour are likely to be adjusted receives illustration from the present position of landlords and tenants: for here the old principles of *laissez faire* and the sacredness of contracts have completely given way to the new collectivist doctrine of State-intervention. It may be that the landlord class which once enjoyed too great power in Parliament, used that power unduly to forward their own interests; and that their successors suffer from a natural reaction that inflicts a new injustice in attempting to redress an old one.

Of the facts, however, there can be no doubt. At elections, twenty tenant votes may be captured for one landlord vote; and no candidate who values his own chances of success can afford to alienate the many to please the few. There will be degrees of cordiality or reluctance; but it would be suicidal openly to favour the landlord class against the tenant class, when a definite issue has been raised between them. Whichever candidate is elected, he is pledged to act as a tenants' friend before he puts foot within St Stephen's.

Here again, the policy that secures the immediate advantage of a class may not contribute to the ultimate prosperity of the nation as a whole. Here again, time must elapse before results are realised in full. Years or even decades may pass before the stream of legislation hostile to house-property diminishes the supply of habitable dwellings relatively to the natural increase of population. Sooner or later, however, the activities of the building trade will be checked, and rents will rise. Tenants, for example, may hail with enthusiasm a measure securing them from eviction during illness; and they may prefer that an occasional malingerer should enjoy the luxury of a rent-free house, rather than that one genuinely sick man should risk losing a boon presented to him by a generous legislature out of the landlord's pocket. If we only wait long enough, however, such malingerers' arrears of rents will automatically distribute themselves over the rents of the other tenants.

Arguments like these, fitted to make powerful appeal to economic theorists sitting leisurely in their armchairs, cannot be expected to produce much effect on aspirants to political honours, or upon the expectant public beneficiaries whose votes they covet. Landlords, once overwhelmingly represented in Parliament, have now no one in the dominant Chamber who dares to champion their unpopular cause. They have no constitutional weapon with which to parry attempts to place exclusively on their shoulders the burden of reforms that ought to be paid for by the whole community.

Owners of real estate have, indeed, fallen on evil days. They have enemies who attack them on grounds of principle, as well as enemies who are mainly actuated by desire to avenge class wrongs of other days. The socialistic attitude is readily understood. Private property in land is immoral and a wrong to the community; it must therefore give way to State-ownership. The displaced wrongdoers deserve no compensation: they do well to escape with nothing worse than mere confiscation of their estates. Several well-known Socialists, indeed, have thought it sufficient expiation for their own past sins in this respect, to realise their hereditary acres at full market values, before joining in the cry for the expropriation of their less far-seeing fellow proprietors, and of those to whom they have sold their estates.

Advocates of the single tax, again, have a somewhat different angle of observation. They have no quarrel with owners of house property, still less with owners of personal estate. To their logic, the peasant's small holding of land is liable to be taxed out of existence equally with the boundless acres of the territorial magnate; while the bank shares of the millionaire are immune. But Socialists and Single-taxers while they thus differ fundamentally in many things, are at one in unqualified hostility towards private property in land. The position of both parties is perfectly logical and consistent. They move steadily towards a conscious goal.

It is more difficult to analyse the attitude of Liberals towards owners of real estate. Few landowners, it is true, whether dukes or peasant proprietors, now support Liberal candidates at elections; but that fact alone would not justify the confiscation of their property. On the other hand, orthodox Liberals invariably repudiate the validity of the arguments put forward by Socialists and Single-taxers. When these arguments are rejected, it is a little difficult to find a theoretical vindication for the State's claim to a share of the "unearned increment" of land; while the dabbler in rubber shares is left to enjoy unmolested the unearned increment of his speculations.

The real justification of this aspect of Liberal finance must be sought in the rapidly increasing national expenditure and the necessity of finding money somewhere. Necessity knows no law; the rights of a few—particularly of a reactionary and recalcitrant few—cannot, it is argued, block the road to great-hearted measures for alleviating the lot of the many. Real estate is the natural prey of the "reformer." Individual landlords in the past have often acted harshly: the entire class has been tactless, selfish, and irritating in its use of political power for party purposes. The resulting odium has passed, like other real burdens on land, to the present owners. A Liberal Government may attack land without fear of alienating its own supporters; for the subscribers to its party war-chest are merchant princes, manufacturers and bankers, rather than country squires. Democracy pays for its triumphs from the purse of its supposed enemies.

IV. *Majorities and Minorities.*

The position of employers and of landlords is by no means unique. All minorities, as such, hold their rights on sufferance. Further illustrations of this general proposition are afforded by the treatment of specially talented artisans under the organised trade-unions. Two classes of wage-earners—minorities, of course—find their interests deliberately sacrificed to the good of their fellows; these are men of special ability, on the one hand, eager to better their lot by increased industry, and, on the other hand, the groups of stunted individuals unable to rise to the minimum standard of efficiency demanded by any one of the organised trades. The position of each of these classes requires separate discussion.

The most valuable form of equality is equality of opportunity. If democracy subordinates the ambitions of artisans of peculiar aptitude to the interests of their indolent, shiftless, and pleasure-loving workmates, it will quickly ruin the prosperity of the nation. Trade-unions, however, are ruled for the benefit of the average members of their rank and file, not of those conspicuous for the qualities that raise men above their fellows. If the House of Commons falls under the same influences, every path of advancement in life for artisan talent will be effectively blocked.

The same influences that bear hardly on superior workmen, fitted to rise above the normal level of mediocrity, bear hardly on those also who sink beneath it. Unskilled labour, not protected by trade-unions, will find itself unrepresented in the democratic parliaments of the future. Casual labourers will be outcasts from the commonwealth, with no effective means of making their voices heard. Every triumph of trade-unionism, whether in raising the minimum wage or in augmenting the stringency of employers' liabilities, increases the growing ranks of the unfit whom no one can afford to employ. These examples may serve to show how all minorities under a democracy are dependent for redress of grievances on the good nature of their legislative masters, who are usually their political opponents. The more bitter the wrong, the less likely is it to be redressed; for the very energy of the victim's struggle to avert disaster will seem irritating contumacy to the ascendant party, and will draw down fresh oppressions as a well-earned punishment.

A minority of nearly half the nation may find itself powerless to modify a single detail of a measure to which it is fiercely opposed. Opinions differ as to the wisdom of the Parliament Act; but no one denies the genuine nature of the detestation felt for it by the millions of voters who opposed it. In a matter of supreme importance, the triumph of the people's will meant, for nearly half the people of Great Britain and for more than half the people of England, the triumph of a measure they abhorred. When organised millions are thus impotent to protect themselves, the abject helplessness of small, unpopular minorities is obvious—unless they are able by some sacrifice of conviction to form an alliance with more numerous forces on the principle of log-rolling. In the late Lord Acton's carefully weighed opinion,[1] "the one pervading evil of democracy is the tyranny of the majority or rather of that party, not always the majority, that succeeds, by force or fraud, in carrying elections."

V. *Majority Rule and National Finance.*

According to Colbert, the whole art of taxation lies in so plucking the goose as to obtain the maximum of down with the minimum of cackling. The authority of a Chancellor of the Exchequer in a modern democracy extends over many millions of geese. He must select for plucking those whose cackling is likely to be least effective; for his title to office depends on the suffrages of the flock. A finance Minister must move along the line of least resistance; he cannot take more than nominal contributions from majorities educated

[1] *Essays on Liberty*, p. 99.

to vote for the leaders who give them most and expect least in return.

Some minorities, indeed, may share in the immunity of majorities, if they are skilful enough to affect the balance between the two great parties that divide the State. In normal circumstances, however, it is on minorities that the heavy hand of a needy Chancellor must fall. Those who have most to fear from the financial needs of a democracy are the unswerving adherents of the defeated party. As the party in power has no hope of winning their support, the full brunt of growing expenditure is sure to fall on them. The friends of democracy have two problems to consider: how far it is desirable to protect such minorities from the vengeful enthusiasm of opponents commanding for the moment the taxing-machinery of the State; and how far it is expedient to allow these minorities, in dread of such attacks, to remove themselves and their belongings to other countries, where they anticipate less unfavourable treatment.

The future of democracy will depend on the nature of the guidance received upon these questions by the sovereign people. Will they be counselled by their responsible lèaders to aim habitually at something higher than the selfish gratification of immediate wants; to obey some voice of conscience, or follow some lofty political ideal? or will they be left without guidance to do what is right in their own eyes, without regard to the claims of abstract justice or the rights of others? Within certain obvious limits, the influence of Ministers in directing public opinion is greater to-day than it has ever been. It is true, of course, that no modern statesman can gain the highest measure of success without making constant concessions to popular demands, and refraining on public platforms from uttering unwelcome truths. The people must be accepted as masters in their own house: political authority is to be gained by anticipating their wishes, not by thwarting them.

It is for Ministers, however, to say in what manner the people's needs shall be supplied. It is for Ministers to settle the thousand and one matters of detail, and to select (always of course with the roll of voters before their eyes) the victims who have to pay the bill. If the people get and get quickly what they want, it matters little to them who finds the money; they have not the leisure, the knowledge, or the patience to analyse the probable consequences to their sons or grandsons of any suggested measure. On all such matters, it is for Ministers to guide public opinion: on their shoulders alone, all responsibility will rest. Ministers then can only guide the people towards what the people want; but it is for the Ministers to choose one from among the various routes.

In the service of the public, a modern Cabinet exercises powers of the widest scope. One House of Parliament has monopolised effective control over taxation and legislation, and that House can be trusted to register automatically the Cabinet's decrees. The party organisation is to-day more perfect, the Whip's power of controlling votes more undoubted than ever before. That modern invention, "closure by compartments," has ground to powder the rights of private members; the doors of the House are closed to all but official candidates of the two great parties; the independent member is a thing of the past. Ministerial power, however, is by no means equally distributed among the members of the Cabinet. It may, indeed, be monopolised by one or two individuals whose popularity makes them indispensable to the party's success at the polls. One man may be able to name his own price, under threat of breaking up the Cabinet. That price will be the more readily agreed to by his less indispensable colleagues, if it has to be paid not out of their own pockets, but out of the national purse.

In money matters, the authority of a really popular and enthusiastic Chancellor of the Exchequer must always have peculiar weight. Under favouring circumstances, the holder of that office might become a practical dictator in the realm of parliamentary finance, and that realm is expanding with a rapidity that brings dizziness to caution-loving heads. Within the elastic lines of the party programme, a framer of the annual budget who retains the confidence of his own party in the Cabinet, the Commons, and the nation, can treat the wealth of millions of his free-born fellow-subjects as no Caliph of Bagdad ever dared to treat the property of his slaves. In the sacred name of the people and of constitutional liberty, he can safely put into motion the inquisitorial authority of Government; while the grinding power of the machinery of taxation at his disposal has been brought to a perfection of smooth-working efficiency never before equalled in any age or country. Under a possible combination of circumstances, the irresistible taxing powers of a one-chambered legislature might be placed at the absolute discretion of one individual Minister of the Crown.

The most timid citizen had no need to dread the vesting of powers so tremendous in the hands of honourable, moderate, and fair-minded statesmen, like those with whom Great Britain has been acquainted in the past; but the possibility of a change occurring in the type of men who are to control the national destinies must not be ignored. It is not difficult to imagine how, in some not far distant age, such a dictatorship might fall to a tribune of the people, whose claims to office were democratic enthusiasm and the power of impassioned, sympathetic, but not necessarily truthful rhetoric, rather than knowledge of economic principles or training in the exacting science of sound national finance.

Our party system makes it possible that some ignorant zealot, claiming as a reward of party services a post for which the Constitution provides no test of fitness, should signalise his entry upon unaccustomed duties, by an attempt to reorganise the economic foundations of society, entering on vast schemes for readjusting, by the scales of his own reason, the unequal balance between rich and poor; without adequate knowledge of the price to be paid by posterity for the violation of natural laws, relying, perhaps, on the second-hand arguments of some pamphlet whose underlying principles he did not fully understand; and who yet found himself strong enough, through the acquiescence of colleagues in the Cabinet, to carry his schemes into operation in face of determined opposition. This may seem a far-fetched and highly-coloured picture, but the day may come when some future historian, looking backward from a safe distance on what is to-day merely ground of speculation, will fill in with definite names and with the details of actual legislative measures the blanks in a sketch that has been here left intentionally vague.

For the present, it is sufficient to note that our constitutional theory and practice provide no test of fitness for aspirants to the post that carries with it control over the tremendous financial powers vested in a modern Chancellor of the Exchequer.

VI. *The Encouragement of Thrift.*

The relations between democratic legislation and thrift—that indispensable foundation of the continued economic pre-eminence of nations—might form the subject for a volume. Thrift, which implies the deliberate sacrifice of immediate gratification in the hope of some gain expected to accrue in the future, has shown itself to be the monopoly of the few. Yet thrift is the philosopher's stone that transmutes the surplus revenue of to-day into the capital of to-morrow: and the accumulation of capital is the prime essential of all permanent advance in the standard of comfort enjoyed by the working classes. It is essential to the well-being of society that the provident minority should not lie at the mercy of the careless or extravagant majority. All expenditure, national or individual, that encroaches on the reserves of capital or discourages additions being made to these, reduces for all time the main source of industrial prosperity. These obvious truisms have led legislators in the past to encourage thrift by all possible expedients, direct or indirect. This has been effected by giving security to property and allowing its free transmission at death by the will of the owner on the one hand; while, on the other hand, the improvident have been left to learn their folly in the hard school of experience.

It is of vital importance to ascertain what attitude is likely to be adopted on this crucial matter by a Parliament professing as its only rule of faith an honest desire to carry out the wishes of the majority. What answer will be forthcoming from the people, asked by Referendum or otherwise, whether they will eat their loaf to-day or reserve it for to-morrow? Would the influence of the self-denying minority induce the mass of their fellow-citizens to sacrifice the present to the future, or their own interests to those of their grandchildren? or will the masses who control legislation, leaning on the boundless philanthropy of a paternal government, more conspicuous for generosity than for discretion, inaugurate a general scramble for the rapidly disappearing fruits of the labours of our forefathers? Will the financial policy of the democracy of the future be ruled by a stern determination to give no encouragement to indolence and improvidence and malingering, or will it be influenced mainly by the desire of candidates to obtain the majority of votes requisite to keep the more virtuous party (that is their own party) in power?

The friends of democracy must be prepared with satisfactory answers to these questions, and be ready to devise a scheme of safeguards, if this should be deemed necessary. One aspect of the wider issue has lately been conspicuous: recent legislation shows a marked bias against all forms of inherited wealth. Hostility in this respect is by no means confined to great fortunes passing at a rich man's death; but is directed against the savings, however modest, of all fathers who have denied themselves for the benefit of their sons. A rich man's heirs, doubtless, can afford to pay toll at reasonable graduated rates on the money they inherit; while the State is justified in protecting itself against the dangers of excessive wealth concentrated in few hands. The payment of a heavy toll on money passing at death ought in fairness to free the ransomed balance of a man's patrimony from further disabilities. This, however, is not the case. Income derived from invested money (that is income that is the result of thrift) is differentiated from what is termed "earned income," and is subjected to further penalties.

Inherited wealth thus pays double toll—first in death duties, and then annually as an additional income tax. The holder of an office of £5000 a year is taxed on a lower scale than the man content to devote himself to scientific or literary pursuits, while he lives in comparative obscurity on an "unearned" income of £1200 a year, the fruit of his own or his father's industry and thrift.

Such attacks upon moderate wealth, inherited from an honourable source, are simply attacks upon self-sacrifice and self-denial: open encouragements to extravagance and improvidence. It is unwise to discourage a man from making comfortable provision for his offspring—a form of saving that may sometimes prove the best method of endowing research;[1] nor is it sound finance to place a penal tax on the moderate income enjoyed in his old age by the man whose youthful energy and forethought have enabled him to retire to a life of innocent leisure on the "unearned" income that represents to him years of strenuous toil.

Parliament ought to encourage thrift. It is quite within its province to diminish the natural handicaps of competitors in the race

[1] *Cf.* A. V. Dicey, *Law and Opinion*, p. 129 *n.*:—"Bentham in this matter resembles Darwin. Each of these eminent men owed to inherited wealth the possibility of wholly dedicating his whole life to its appropriate work."

of life, so as to give each man a decently fair start; but it must not try so to arrange the weights that all, independent of individual effort, shall arrive simultaneously at the goal. It is not its business to restrain the swift so that he shall not outstrip the slow; or to give to the athlete who stops at each refreshment bar equal chance of victory with the competitor who runs straight on.

VII. *The Value of Individual Liberty.*

Liberty is no longer the word to conjure with in English politics that once it was. John Stuart Mill and Herbert Spencer are no longer the apostles of the party of progress. Some of the older advocates of the gospel of freedom of action may, indeed, by a tendency to overstatement, have discredited its own claims. Under the reign of *laissez faire*, men and women too often found their abstract political freedom accompanied by economic slavery under the pressure of conditions they were powerless to resist. Nominal freedom of contract confers no real liberty on the starving wretch who is compelled to accept the only conditions offered him to satisfy his daily recurring wants. It was necessary that legislation should set limits to the horrors of a regime of absolute non-intervention.

It may be well to ask whether the pendulum

has not swung too far to the opposite extreme. In two directions, the freedom of action of the individual working-man is increasingly contracted; by the intervention of a paternal government anxious to regulate his life after that government's own ideals rather than his own; and by the growing power of trade-unions to coerce their own members and non-unionists who interfere with trade-union policy.

The House of Commons which, if it interferes at all, ought to prevent the weak from being bullied by the strong, has shown its readiness to conciliate organised labour by conferring privileged treatment in respect of liabilities incurred through actions of doubtful legality, and by protecting picketers in intimidating "blacklegs," up to the verge of violence. The freedom of the artisan of superior intelligence and energy is ruthlessly sacrificed to the interests of the generality. Within trade-unions, equality and fraternity may reign; but liberty is extinct.

Parliament, however, not content with encouraging tyranny in others, is itself a tyrant—though a tyrant with the utmost benevolence of intention. Every police borough has its own special statutory powers for enforcing the network of minute regulations with which it hedges round the life of its citizens. While professors of law continue to teach their students, in formulas familiar from the days of Blackstone, that English law is entirely favourable to the presumption of liberty of individual action and initiative, as a matter of fact arbitrary powers are being accumulated by magistrates and by the police with an alarming rapidity.

Nor is this all; the whole spirit and motives of general legislation have suffered a complete change. It is no longer admitted that the individual should be master of his own destiny; that he best knows what he wants and has a right to attempt to get it in his own way; that every interference of the state with his initiative is a wrong to him and likely to do more harm than good. These truths, once accepted as the whole gospel of constitutional progress, are now utterly discarded. Not only is the right of contract much curtailed, but the provision a man must make for sickness or misfortune is regulated by statute. This method of treating the adult working-man may perhaps be necessary in the interests of the more shiftless minority, but it cannot be denied that it is treating him like a child. No ideals could be at more complete variance with those of the Liberal party in the days when Great Britain started on a career of prosperity, which has raised its working classes to a standard of comfort still considerably in advance of that of any other country in Europe.

It may not be useless to ask the question whether the new attitude of the Legislature towards the working-man, of treating him frankly as an inferior being, not able to take care of himself and his children, may not foster in him a habit of dependence on a fatherly government, and thus undermine, sooner or later, the characteristic of self-reliance upon which England's greatness has mainly depended. If a man is habitually treated like a child, he may in time become as helpless as a child. The value of individual liberty may have been overestimated in the past; but it cannot be safely eliminated from the list of ingredients of social progress; while as Mr Harold Cox reminded us the other day,[1] "of all individual liberties none is more important, both for the individual himself and for the community of which he is a part, than the right of a man to use to the best advantage his abilities as a wealth-producer." The country that crushes out private initiative by imposing unnecessarily hampering restrictions on the actions of its citizens, will quickly decline among the nations.

[1] *Nineteenth Century*, September 1911, p. 419.

CHAPTER IV

THE STUMBLING BLOCKS OF DEMOCRACY

DEMOCRACY takes many forms. It would be folly to contend that all of these are equally worthy of trust and admiration. There are degrees of excellence among them equally as among other forms of government. Each has its own dangers, although some dangers may be common to all.

I. *The Difficulty of Plain Speaking.*

One evil of democracies is undoubted: it is impossible for a successful politician to tell "the truth, the whole truth, and nothing but the truth" to a popular audience on whose votes he depends for his career. Other types of government are subject in varying measure to similar dangers. Plain speaking is apt to be resented by monarchs and oligarchs alike. Flattery is the courtier's only road to favour; but the court of King Demos has features that distinguish it from those of other sovereigns.

To begin with, toleration of unpleasant advice is the virtue of the few; the most incorrigible of optimists would not expect a crowd of average labourers to welcome the plain, unvarnished truth. The counsellors of monarchs, indeed, have sometimes found the highest form of selfish wisdom to consist in silence; but even the most despotic of medieval kings allowed his jester to speak the truth, when other mouths were shut. No licensed fool holds the ear of King Demos to warn him of faults and limitations. The politician who advises the sovereign people to sacrifice their own present gratification for the benefit of posterity will have a short career.

In the debates on the Minimum Wage Bill in the House of Commons on 21st March 1912, only faint voices were raised for the repeal of the Trade Disputes Act, which enlightened opinion outside the House was unanimous in condemning. The increasing difficulties that, in the House of Commons, or on the election platform, prevent the expression of the full honest truth, constitute a danger of the first magnitude. Men of science who write learned books, may dare to explain their real convictions to the insignificant minority who read them; but the masses who control elections are guided by appeals of a different type. Walter Bagehot, writing soon after the Reform Act of 1867, has said "as a theoretical writer, I can venture to say what no elected

Member of Parliament, Conservative or Liberal, can venture to say, that I am exceedingly afraid of the ignorant multitude of the new constituencies."[1] In 1912, candidates for election, bound to humour that multitude to the top of its bent, look back with envy to the comparative independence of forty years ago. Those whom the masses follow are not writers of thoughtful books like Bagehot, but makers of inflammatory speeches, pointing out panaceas for the redress of real or fancied wrongs. The people, organised in their trade-unions and syndicates, listen only to two types of advisers: to professional labour leaders and to politicians who cajole them in order to obtain their votes. The undiluted truth is a stream of which the electors have little chance to drink.

II. *The Policy of Doles.*

Candidates, who take their chances of election seriously, must do more than merely colour facts to please their audience; they must promise more tempting gifts than their opponents. The man who dangles the most attractive bait will catch most fish. This danger of democracies was foreseen by Bagehot's prophetic eye: "I can conceive of nothing more corrupting or worse for a set of poor, ignorant people than that

[1] Introduction, p. xxix.

two combinations of well-taught and rich men should constantly offer to defer to their decision, and compete for the office of executing it. *Vox populi* will be *vox diaboli* if it is worked in that manner."[1]

Events have moved rapidly since 1872: the scope of legislation and the means of corrupting the voters have developed amazingly. Experience has confirmed Bagehot's worst fears, and has revealed dangers by him unsuspected, for to-day one of the two parties habitually outbids the other, while the outdistanced competitor keeps pathetically offering pennies against the shillings promised by its rival. Where a permanent monopoly of power exists, the evils of party government are perpetuated without its compensating advantages. A Government always in office would be unhampered by the need of moderation or the spirit of compromise, and so might defy hostile criticism and treat the remonstrances of its victims with contempt. Such conditions are exceptional: one party cannot permanently be excluded from office. If lavish bribes are offered by one side, counter bribes will be offered by the other. Power will pass backwards and forwards from the party that for the moment hesitates and counts the cost to that which promises the maximum of concession to the most numerous class of voters.

[1] Introduction, p. xxiii.

The contest, once entered on, is obviously one in which the prize must always go to the most incautious and the most unscrupulous. Sound national finance becomes impossible.

Another recent development of the party system threatens a return to the worst practices of the reigns of William of Orange and Queen Anne. In that period of faction and party spite it was usual, on a change of Government, for the new Ministers to inaugurate their term of office by impeaching their predecessors. In similar circumstances in the twentieth century, the leaders of the defeated party are immune from criminal procedure; but their property is liable to attack. The party that gains control over the machinery of taxation celebrates its victory by imposing burdens on the property of the vanquished minority, if that property can be singled out for separate attack. No secret was made of the intention to penalise the landed aristocracy by means of the Finance Act of 1909, for the conduct of the House of Lords in using their legal powers to destroy the Education and Licensing Bills. The same measure that punished the Ministry's chief opponents was intended to reward their supporters, by lightening their share of taxation, and by providing a fund for the relief of their humbler members.

These new methods of influencing elections do not fall under the ban of the various Acts against corrupt practices, for the bribes are conferred on classes of voters and not on individuals. The wholesale method of buying votes is far more effective than the older, timid methods which penal statutes were effectual to restrain. It is also more ingenious, for the money needed to undermine the integrity of the electors is derived not from the pockets of those who profit by it, but from the national purse.

Once such methods have been adopted by either party, it is useless to speak of turning back. Voters, habituated to receiving annually increasing doles, with the assurance that these are less than is their due, are unlikely to look with favour upon candidates who have nothing more succulent to offer than good advice and wholesome but unwelcome facts about the possibility of national bankruptcy threatening in the future.

III. *The Ignorance of the Masses.*

These dangers are the greater because of the complex conditions of modern life and the expansion of the province of legislative activity. Even in a small and homogeneous state like Switzerland, the electors find it difficult to keep themselves informed on the issues submitted to them. The ignorance that is inseparable from popular legislation, is ten-fold more hurtful in dealing with the affairs of a scattered empire, with tangled interests in every part of the habitable globe. British voters have no possibility of acquiring the encyclopædic knowledge necessary to form independent judgments on the questions that come before the Imperial Parliament. They have their living to make, whether as colliers, grocers, or unskilled labourers, as physicians, engineers, or bankers; and therefore ignorance, bearing with it no stigma or reproach, is the necessary condition of the great mass of electors of the upper and middle as well as of the lower classes. Only specialists, within their own limited spheres of thought and labour, are competent to decide on the wisdom or folly of legislative measures bearing on their own subjects.

In these circumstances, it is doubly deplorable that candidates for election should mould "the will of the people" with half-truths or deliberate misstatements, or should divert attention from wider issues by harping on the immediate gain to be reaped by the individual voter. It is deplorable that each side should promise a bigger loaf for the same standard price. Ignorant multitudes know the bitterness of their own needs, but know nothing of their causes; and but little of the difficulties and dangers that surround all suggested methods for relieving them. They can by no means be trusted to select the alternative that is least likely to inflict injustice on individuals, or to bequeath injury to posterity. If left to their own guidance, they will take the straightest and most wasteful course to the immediate satisfaction of their wants.

IV. *The Dethronement of* Laissez Faire.

During the nineteenth century, the chief battles of progress and reform were fought and won under the banner of *laissez faire.* John Stuart Mill and Herbert Spencer preached to willing ears the doctrine of a strictly limited sphere of Government intervention. Followers of Adam Smith were firmly convinced that natural laws were too strong for Acts of Parliament to control. Liberal politicians were more strenuous than Conservatives in condemning as economically unsound the attempts of medieval legislators to regulate prices and wages and the conditions of labour by Act of Parliament. Radicals of a by-gone age narrowed the province of Government to the duties of preserving peace, enforcing contracts, and keeping a clear field for the competitors in the race of life: all unnecessary interference with individual rights and liberties was regarded as sin.

All this is changed: these old-fashioned doctrines have been discarded with contumely. The reaction from a regime of unbridled *laissez faire* has not rested content with the provisions of such excellent statutes as the Factory Acts. The Legislature has gone further and further in the direction of State-intervention, until there is no hole or cranny in the national life into which it has not penetrated. In the twentieth century Parliament is rapidly reverting to the medieval conception (until lately overwhelmed with universal ridicule) that Government can regulate the prices of commodities and the wages of labour without regard to the natural laws that control the labour market. So sweeping an extension of the province of the Legislature may be fraught with grave consequences. Once the principle of a minimum wage fixed by Parliament has been conceded, few wage-earners are likely to cast their votes for the party promising an increase of only 3d in the day's wage as against the party willing to authorise a halfpenny more.

V. *Extravagance of the House of Commons.*

The same House of Commons that has made good its claims to legislative sovereignty, unlimited in range and extent, has long been noted for extravagant tendencies. In its Standing Orders, indeed, it has attempted to make provision against its own admitted habits of lavish outlay at the public expense: no supply can be voted except on the invitation of a Minister of the Crown, who thus assumes responsibility for the expenditure incurred, and no financial measure will be discussed before the Commons have resolved themselves into a committee of the whole House.

The reasons for these precautions are obvious: each Member of Parliament prefers to obtain popularity by bestowing gifts upon A, rather than to incur the hostility of B by opposing doles suggested by others; while the mere principle of "economy" is too cold an abstraction to have much influence in gaining votes. A cheese-paring policy in dealing with public money must be unpopular in an age when all distressed or discontented classes are taught to look confidently to Parliament for relief. When all mouths are agape for the food dispensed by a bountiful Government, a reputation for making lavish grants will open the door to the highest offices in the State.

Recent events have not increased confidence in the economy of the House of Commons; for the 670 gentlemen who compose it have celebrated the statutory confirmation of their claim to act as sole guardians of the public purse by immediately appropriating £268,000 to their private needs, without waiting for the constitutional formalities necessary to the passing of a Money Bill in usual form. This sum is to be regarded merely as one year's salary, and it fixes their minimum wage for the future; but these trusty custodians of the national Exchequer have been successful in demonstrating that the Constitution contains no machinery to prevent them from rewarding themselves for their own services to the nation in coming years, by voting themselves salaries at much higher rates. The labourer is worthy of his hire; and it is perhaps not unreasonable that those who dispense among their supporters so many millions of public money, should deduct a reasonable commission as an honorarium for their own services.

After all, mere formalities are of little importance when it is realised that *all* constitutional restraints have been removed that once stood between the Government and the property of the governed. The party machinery enables the individuals who dominate the Cabinet to dominate also the only effective part of the Legislature. Whether they proceed by Resolution or by the more usual constitutional method of Statute, the result is practically the same—the wealth of a great empire lies as a rich spoil at the mercy of the party majority that controls Executive Government and House of Commons alike.

Here, again, the constitutional safeguards of individual rights and liberties have failed to act. Originally devised to protect the subject against a tyrant king; they now place him absolutely at the mercy of a tyrant Parliament, a benevolent and just tyrant possibly, but a tyrant still. The distribution of public money among the Commons, by Resolution of their own House without statutory authority, affords a new illustration of the difference between the theory and practice of our Constitution. The motives prompting the majority of the Commons to this step have been, doubtless, of the loftiest and most disinterested kind; but the fact that in their hour of triumph over the other House, they should have made themselves the first object of the national bounty they dispense, does not render the transaction the less noteworthy.

VI. *Effects of Unstable Economic Conditions.*

An era of legislation is an era of change. The ease and frequency with which the conditions that regulate men's lives are altered, have produced a fluid state of society. Each morning, the man with any established interest in which he has staked capital or industry, opens his newspaper with dread, lest the conditions on which success depends have been dissipated in the night. Parliamentary bills, it is true, still require three readings; but many a business, the fruit of a life's labours, may be ruined by the insertion of an amendment in an ill-digested measure, inadequately discussed in the House of Commons or not discussed at all.

The foundations of society no longer rest on pillars of adamant. A framework, woven out of gossamers dangling in the air, has taken the place of the old cast-iron system that enforced all contractual obligations and safeguarded vested rights. Such a condition of things, interesting as it is to observers at a safe distance, is appalling to those who realise that the continued prosperity of society depends on credit, and that in turn depends on a sense of stability and security.

Capital, while it may be confiscated, cannot be dispensed with; and capital will melt away, if it is unprotected. Unlike land and houses, which are immovable and therefore easy victims of predatory legislation, personal estate is free to seek the country most favourable to its prosperity. When the moneyed classes come to realise their helplessness against a House of Commons controlled by organised wage-earners, the exodus of capital, conspicuous since 1909, will be rapidly accelerated. While British industries thus suffer through the withdrawal of the existing wealth that is scared abroad, they will suffer further through loss of the potential capital that might have been available but for the fatal policy of substituting State aid for thrift and self-reliance. Capital will not accumulate in the pockets of the artisan or small trader, if he is taught that those who spend and afterwards rely on the eleemosynary grants of a philanthropic

State, do better for themselves than those who rely on their own forethought and energy. Among the masses, who control the destinies of democracies, there is a tendency, natural enough but deplorable in its effects, to dissipate the painfully accumulated reserves of national capital in an attempt to satisfy the ever-pressing needs of a rising standard of living, combined with the ever-increasing burden of maintaining the prolific submerged class. Democracy not only frightens capital from the country, but squanders part of what is left at home.

These tendencies combine with the feeling of insecurity they engender, to produce a thoroughly unhealthy economic condition. No nation can successfully compete with its ever-wakeful rivals, if the feeling becomes general that the Government and its subservient legislature cannot be trusted to protect private property, or to guard from meddlesome interference industries that depend on credit and stability of economic conditions. A wise democracy that looks even a few years ahead, must be watchful to allay the suspicions of those who have power to increase or diminish the amount of capital at the service of national industries. The only alternative policy would seem to be the immediate acceptance by the Legislature (without warning to its victims) of the entire Socialist programme of nationalising all forms of capital, and thus placing an absolute embargo on the emigration of capital—a policy more easily suggested than carried into effect.

VII. *Influence of Democracy on the Economic Future of the Nation.*

The probable effect of democracy in the remote future must be weighed, alongside of its more immediate results. After a few generations have enjoyed the beneficent sway of a completely democratic government, acting as an open-handed terrestrial providence, will Great Britain be more or less prosperous than it has been under a less optimistic and more parsimonious regime? What consequences will the new spirit produce (*a*) on the economic future of the nation; (*b*) on the moral fibre of the citizen; (*c*) on the problems of population and Eugenics?

The change from a regime of self-help and private enterprise to one of State-aid and legislative intervention, must powerfully affect the production, as well as the distribution, of wealth. What effects are likely to be produced on those habits of saving and self-denial, on which the accumulation of capital depends, by the expectation that the needy will be sympathetically relieved of the consequences of their own improvidence? Will the working of the constitutional machinery under the new conditions, be such as to ensure the husbanding of national resources? Are sufficient checks provided to restrain the extravagant tendencies of the House of Commons? Are the conditions that determine the selection of a Chancellor of the Exchequer, as practical dictator of national expenditure, such as to ensure his qualifications as a master of sound finance rather than of persuasive eloquence? Is his tenure of office so regulated, that it will act as a guarantee that public money shall never be spent with the object of gaining votes or of punishing his political opponents, but always for the lasting benefit of the commonwealth? What is the effect on national finance of the abolition of all those checks and balances for which the British Constitution once was famous? What, again, are the probable effects of wages artificially fixed at higher rates than those of foreign competitors, and of the burden of taxation for providing salaries for the hordes of inspectors and Government officials?

Is there a breaking point beyond which the burden of rates and taxes and of expensive statutory requirements cannot go without disabling the staple industries of the country? or are our resources so exceptional that no foreign nation, working under cheap conditions, can possibly filch away our trade? Will the more progressive and abler artisans be content to accept the restraints placed on their freedom of action by trade unions conducted, and legislation passed in the interests of inferior working-men? Will they submit to regulations framed to prevent them earning the full wage their abilities are fit to earn? Will they allow their chances of rising in life to be taken from them; or will the exodus of the picked men of various industries, already known to have begun from the Thames, the Clyde and the Mersey, be likely to continue and increase?

These are only a few of the questions that must be answered by anyone who would forecast the future of British industry and commerce, when the new democracy has come into its own. The mere asking of them may not be without its uses, since many of the measures placed on our Statute-Rolls seem to proceed on the assumption that no such problems exist.

VIII. *The Influence of Democracy on National Character.*

Men are more valuable than material wealth. Even from a purely economic standpoint, the most precious part of a nation's assets consists in the health, happiness, and uprightness of its individual men and women. The all-important question thus arises:—What will be the ultimate effect of modern democratic legislation on the national character? If a better, hardier, more self-reliant race of men is to be reared to take their fathers' places in the next generation, then there is the less need to scan with miserly care the anticipated bill of costs.

While the increased expenditure, however, is a certainty, the return for the money spent is more problematical. It is sometimes maintained that the lavish methods of democratic finance tend to relax rather than to give tone to the moral fibre of the nation. The individual has now less need to depend on his own exertions for maintenance, comfort, and security in life. A paternal State steps in between his improvidence and its natural consequences in the stern discipline of life. Errors of judgment or of conduct are no longer left, in the callous manner of an earlier age, to bring their own retribution. A healing ointment is provided for every smart by the nation's accredited almoners, at the expense of the prudent and well-behaved. Depending on the community for the education and even for the food and clothing of the children he has brought into the world, ensured by Act of Parliament against sickness, unemployment, and all the vicissitudes of life at his employer's and the State's expense, entitled to heavy damages for injuries caused by his own carelessness, and with an absolute claim to a pension in old age, the individual is relieved of most of the responsibilities of life. With mind relieved from care for the morrow, he is free to step jauntily along the path of life, spending his earnings as he goes.

The respective spheres of State-action and individual-action have thus been entirely re-adjusted. The individual has only to get himself born: the State will do the rest. The community will watch over him from his cradle to his grave. It is useless to pretend that there is no darker side to this picture. A community, after all, is composed of individuals: and responsibility cannot be got rid of by simply transferring it to the State. A condition of society under which millions of shiftless and spendthrift wastrels are encouraged to repudiate all liability for themselves and their families, and in which poverty, as such, is recognised as an absolute claim to relief, is full of dangers. "If poor men," says Mr Harold Cox,[1] "are to be helped out of public funds simply because they are poor, poverty will become by itself a title to pecuniary reward; and the result will be that the main motive for industrial effort will disappear."

Every well-meant measure that stands between the improvident and the consequences of his own improvidence is bound to have evil effects. Against the obvious

[1] *Nineteenth Century*, September 1911, p. 421.

merits, for example, of the scheme of old age pensions, must be reckoned its effect on the natural unwillingness of men to disqualify themselves for its receipt by laying past provision for their own old age. When a man is relieved of his own natural responsibilities, he is emptied of the qualities that make for manhood—of independence, initiative, self-control, self-reliance, and self-sacrifice. If the destruction of these characteristics is the sole return to the State for its lavish expenditure, democratic legislation is doing worse than merely wasting the material wealth of the community: it is undermining the national character. It is doing its best to eradicate from the next generation of Britons the qualities that have enabled their forefathers to build up the British Empire. England, however, is merely on the threshold of her great experiments in paternal government. More than one generation will have passed away before its full effects can be appreciated.

IX. *Influence of Democratic Legislation on Population.*

A democracy that insists on equal rights for all its citizens has special need to protect itself against the entrance of the ineligible. It is not enough to close its harbours to the undesirable alien: the gates of population must be guarded. Every obstacle must be placed in the way of the morally worthless propagating their kind. While the reckless breeding of the incompetent and diseased is thus checked, energetic and deserving citizens should be encouraged to improve the average of the national stock by rearing families to inherit their own qualities, and to profit by the stored up fruits of their exertions and abstinence.

The problems of the science of Eugenics, still in its infancy, cannot be here discussed. One obvious truth, however, may be insisted on. Everything that interferes with parental responsibility is an unmixed evil. It relaxes the moral fibre of the present generation, and increases the morally worthless members of the next. If men are to be encouraged to bring children into the world, and then freed from the obligation to feed and clothe them, a rapid deterioration in the physical, mental, and moral qualities of the English race is inevitable. Unfortunately, this is precisely the effect of the great mass of well-meaning philanthropic legislation of the present day. It is natural enough for a kind-hearted, if somewhat sentimental, public to insist on the cruelty and absurdity of trying to educate a hungry child. It is a natural corollary that proper food, clothing and medical attendance should be provided from the public purse. It need not be forgotten, however, that the nation that commits itself to such a policy, has a price to pay that is by no means confined to the mere pecuniary outlay. The bill of costs includes the rapid increase of the submerged class, the multiplication of individuals unwilling or unable to help themselves, clinging therefore like a millstone round the necks of the more deserving.

Such a policy means the survival of the most unfit; for it makes the prudent and self-dependent citizen unwilling to add to the increasing burdens of life by producing children whom he will have to maintain on his own higher plane without State-aid, in addition to maintaining the children of his prolific riff-raff neighbours. The cautious man, accustomed to pay his own way, will hesitate to undertake the responsibilities of marriage, under a legislature that puts increasing difficulties in the path of the progressive minority, and makes increasing demands upon his purse for the children of idlers and malingerers.

Among the successful and ambitious classes, early marriages become more rare, large families become fewer, while unions entirely childless are more frequent. Under modern conditions, few fathers may hope to leave sufficient means to help their children to take as good an economic position as their parents have done. Increased death duties, income taxes, and local rates, combined with the feeling of insecurity caused among small capitalists and property owners by the trend of democratic legislation, add new reasons for the steady diminution in the birth-rate among the well-to-do. The steady workman who has saved a little money, and is taxed for the benefit of the numerous progeny of his wastrel neighbours, can the less afford the luxury of a family of his own. The same legislation that increases the birth-rate of the debased, checks the birth-rate of the deserving. The democracy of the future, unless some antidote is devised, will be distinguished more for the quantity than the quality of its citizens. The competent and prudent will shrink from the responsibilities of fatherhood, which their manhood dares not disown; while the worthless, whose repudiation of responsibility has been endorsed by the State, will multiply and replenish the earth.

These are only a few of the stumbling blocks in the path of popular government. Enough has been said to show that democracy, like other forms of government, has dangers of its own — dangers which its well-wishers would be unwise to ignore. Democracy which, with its noble ideals, promises for the toiling millions a new heaven and a new earth, must be carefully guarded from becoming in practice a hell in which the degraded and diseased have choked out the healthy and progressive. A depraved democracy would be the worst of tyrants: for it has no reverse of fortune to fear. A monarch trembles lest he should be deposed or slain; an oligarchy lest it should be stript of its monopolies; but the Demos is strong in the assurance that it has everything to gain and nothing to lose by revolutionary measures. "The people at large," said Burke, "can never become the object of punishment by any human hand." A form of polity, which its apostle Rousseau characterised as a government for gods and unfit for men, and which has been described in less complimentary terms by Bagehot[1] as "the supremacy of ignorance over instruction and of numbers over knowledge," may mean in practice the vesting of supreme authority in, what Mr Joseph Conrad calls, "the stupid brutality of crowds."

[1] Introduction, pp. xxiii. xxiv.

CHAPTER V

THE THEORETICAL BASIS OF DEMOCRACY

Two doctrines lie at the root of popular government: the political equality of all members of a State, and the right of the majority to rule.

I. *Assumption of Equality.*

The belief that every citizen, whatever his abilities or equipment, ought to have an equal weight in determining the national policy may be examined either from the point of view of the body politic or from that of the individual. The community is a corporate whole, and its corporate will is something different from the sum of the isolated particular wills of the individuals who compose it. If 51 per cent. of the population support a measure because it promises to put a few more pence per annum into the pocket of each of them while it spells ruin to the other 49 per cent., and is opposed on principle by the numerically unimportant body of expert opinion, that measure cannot, in any accurate sense, be said to be in accordance with the "will" of the nation. What a progressive community effectively desires to have, and what is best for it to have, cannot be ascertained by a mere balancing of the Ayes against the Noes. Quantity becomes an unreal abstraction when it is altogether divorced from quality. In the words of a recent writer on constitutional liberty in Hungary:[1] "To the question which class should predominate, the answer often is the largest class, the democratic element. This, however, is a mistake. It is not numbers which should tell, but moral weight."

The sanctity of the principle of equality is also open to attack from the side of the individual. The assumption that, in determining the national will, all particular wills count alike has been hotly contested. In every old community, as Bagehot[2] maintains, the primitive and guiding assumption of democracy "is at war with truth. By its theory all people are entitled to the same political power, and they can only be so entitled on the ground that in politics they are equally wise."

This is not a party question. Liberals, with their ideals of "one man one vote," and Con-

[1] Count Andrassy, *Development of Hungarian Liberty*, p. 165.

[2] Page 263.

servatives, with their demand for equal electoral divisions and their belief in a popular Referendum, are equally accelerating our rate of progress towards a form of polity only to be justified on a purely "atomistic" conception of society.

The democratic theory of equality, which founds citizenship on the conception of rights rather than of duties, claims for the ignorant and shiftless an equal title to rule the State with those who are endowed with moral force and have acquired the necessary mental equipment.

It is different in the actual world of affairs, for there inequality is the invariable rule. A system of government which assumes the political equality of beings who are radically unequal in all important respects, is as untenable in theory as it is dangerous in practice.

(1) *Political and Economic Equality.*—"Equality" is a word of many ambiguities; for there are various kinds of equality. If the theoretical basis of democracy be admitted, that men of unequal value, physically, intellectually, and morally, should have equal voting power, it would still remain to be asked how far this theory of political equality involves the admission of equality in other respects. Does political equality, for example, tend to bring financial equality in its wake? On this point there

seems little room for doubt. If sovereign power is equally distributed among twenty millions of men, voting more or less on selfish individualistic principles, they will naturally try to obtain a more equal distribution of material comfort. If they succeed in this attempt, economists contend that, by removing the incentive of gain and by destroying the productive power of capital through its dissipation, the result will be not universal comfort but universal poverty.

If it is thought desirable that such attempts at levelling wealth should fail, then constitutional expedients to effect that end ought to be devised. These might take one of three forms: the deliberate denial of political equality by the establishment of a system of graduated voting power; the limitation of the sphere of parliamentary activity; or the invention of machinery for placing delays and difficulties in the path of financial legislation. All three methods are equally opposed to present-day tendencies, and are unlikely to find support. It must therefore be assumed that in Great Britain, unlike the United States of America where safeguards exist, political equality is sure to bring material equality in its train.

While accepting this result as inevitable when once political equality has been established, it may not be unprofitable to discuss the underlying principles. Does either justice or expediency demand an equal division of the national revenue among all the citizens, irrespective of their past conduct or forethought, and of their ability to use wealth for good purposes in the future? If a select few of a body of artisans, for example, accumulate a moderate reserve fund out of surplus wages which their fellows prefer to spend in drink, ought the improvident majority, keeping rigidly to the letter of the law of equality, be allowed to compel a redistribution of the fund thus accumulated? Obviously, reserves of capital could never be built up, if the savings of thrifty minorities were not protected from danger of immediate confiscation by the legislature in order to allay the thirst of spendthrift majorities. The circumstances suggested, however, will be readily admitted to form an extreme case. Capitalists on a large scale, it may be urged, are in a different position. Their wealth may be the result neither of their own superior industry nor of their own self-denial. It has come to them in the night-time while they slept. It may have taken the form of a bequest by a rich father, or be the result of unfair economic conditions that diverted to the pockets of the indolent, revenues earned by the unremitting toil of their less fortunate fellow-citizens. This is an extreme case on the other side.

Capital, however it may have been acquired, is not in itself an evil to the community. It may be pointed out, by those who would defend its existence against democratic demands, that much of the present stock of capital has been honestly acquired by the hands or brains of those who still possess it; that all forms of wealth in private hands, particularly inherited wealth, pay heavy and frequent toll to the needs of the community; that national prosperity is dependent on the continuance of a widespread feeling of security; and, finally, that the present generation of wage-earners would have been in a much worse plight than they are at present, if all past revenue had been widely dispersed and spent by the many, instead of being allowed to accumulate in the hands of the few. From the point of view of succeeding generations, there is a wide difference between wealth hoarded and wisely invested on the one hand, and, on the other, wealth distributed so as to increase the birth-rate among the least provident classes of society.

It would thus seem that, even on the assumption of a fundamental equality among all the citizens of a State, there is no law of justice or of social expediency that necessarily calls for the condemnation of capital. Economic equality is not logically involved in political equality; but the two tend in practice to go hand-in-hand, and that tendency is a source of danger to the well-being of the State, in which the well-being of the industrial classes is necessarily bound up. Labour must suffer from any legislation that diminishes the capital on which industrial development depends.

(2) *Other Aspects of Equality.*—Strict adherence to the theory of political equality has an unfavourable effect on the development of certain other kinds of equality. The form of equality that flourishes least under popular government is one which is by no means a democratic monopoly, but is an essential feature in every well-regulated community. "Equality before the law" is the most obvious and indispensable variety of all. The "rule of law" is one of three fundamental principles of the British Constitution; and it implies that there is one law for rich and poor, for officials and private citizens. No privileges are allowed to any individual, corporation, or institution.

Quite recently, in Great Britain, under the pressure of the massed Labour vote, this principle has been abandoned. The Trade Disputes Act has placed in the hands of trade unions, when engaged in a struggle with their employers, privileges which elsewhere are admittedly illegal. Political equality, a principle whose credentials are at best doubtful, has thus led to an infringement of the principle of "equality before the law," which lies at the basis of all orderly government. The same Trade Disputes Act has also encroached on two other forms of equality: on equality of liberty and equality of opportunity. The non-union labourer or the "blackleg" unionist, who claims the right to labour when a majority of his fellows have decided on a strike, finds himself incapable of resistance in the artificial circumstances created by a legislature that has taken sides against him. By conceding the right of "peaceful picketing" to those who desire to use it as a screen for threats of open violence, the Act of 1906 has deprived minorities of their right to equality of opportunity. Legislation, forced upon a government by "political equality," has proved fatal to more essential aspects of that principle.

One kind of equality, however, tends to be produced by the equality of voting power enjoyed by members of trade unions: equality of wage is insisted on in the interests of the worker of average abilities. The artisan of superior energy and abilities is not allowed to earn a bigger wage than his fellows by increasing his daily output. The pace of all is set by the capacity of the slowest; and the loss falls partly on the community through the employees, but mainly on the able artisan who is sacrificed for the advantage of those less competent.

It is interesting to note that democratic doctrine, while founding its claims on the theory of equality, and ready to press that theory to extremities where its purposes are suited (as, for example, in the demand for an equal distribution of wealth, and in the attempt to restrict workers of unequal capacity to an equal output), is yet ready enough, on occasion, to abandon it when inconvenient. Equality of opportunity is denied to non-unionists in search of work; and the rights of aliens and subject races are never allowed to come into serious conflict with the aspirations of the average British working-man.

II. *The Basis of Majority Rule.*

The right of majorities to demand and obtain precisely what they want is usually accepted as axiomatic. It rarely occurs, even to theorists, to question the historical basis of the claim, or to require the justification on grounds of logic, utility, or common sense of a principle everywhere taken on trust. There is no good reason, however, why these questions should not be asked. Why should the freedom, property, and lives of nearly half the nation lie, absolutely without appeal, at the mercy of the other half? Would any sane man, who has anything to lose, voluntarily join a society whose members have the right by secret voting to strip him of all he has? Majority rule in its modern form cannot expect to pass unchallenged; like other institutions of human origin, it may, without offence, be asked for its credentials.

(1) *Historical Basis.*—An inquiry into the origin and development of the doctrine may prove that, after all, it is of comparatively modern invention—that, at least, it is not an "innate" idea or one that finds favour with primitive man. The practice of deciding disputed questions of policy by the simple device of counting heads, took its rise in England, as a rule of convenience necessary to the smooth working of the system of representative institutions.

In England it was first resorted to apparently in the thirteenth century; but then and for long afterwards it was used only as a temporary expedient to be applied timidly and tentatively. Its first conspicuous appearance would seem to be that contained in the famous executive clause of King John's Great Charter.[1] The article of which this clause forms part (c. 61 of *Magna Carta*), after conferring on a committee of twenty-five barons wide powers for compelling the King to observe the provisions of the Charter, thus proceeds: "If perchance those twenty-five are present and disagree about anything, or if some of them after being summoned, are unwilling or unable to be present, that which the majority of those present ordain or

[1] *Cf.* Mr Baty in *Quarterly Review,* January 1912.

command shall be held as fixed and established, exactly as if the whole twenty-five had concurred in this."[1] This enunciation of the principle of majority rule, as a temporary expedient for meeting a special difficulty, should be read in connection with a clause contained in another article of the same charter. Article 14 provides for the method of summoning a Common Council (or embryo Parliament) to authorise the taking of aids or scutages (the two normal forms of feudal grants) from the crown vassals, and thus concludes: "When the summons has thus been made, the business shall proceed on the day appointed, according to the counsel of such as are present, although not all who are summoned have come."[2] As is well known, both of these clauses bearing on the rights of majorities to bind present or absent minorities, were omitted from all re-issues and confirmations of *Magna Carta.*[3]

The extreme inconvenience of requiring absolute unanimity, apparently, forced the barons in 1215 to recognise the decision of a majority as having the force of a decision of the whole body of twenty-five: the circumstances were in every way exceptional. The practice, however, of compelling minorities to join in paying imposts at the grant of which they had been present and

[1] See McKechnie, *Magna Carta,* p. 548.
[2] *Ibid.,* p. 292. [3] *Ibid.,* p. 166.

protested against, was not yet thought of. In 1221, Peter des Roches, Bishop of Winchester, repudiated liability for his due proportion of a scutage (or feudal levy) granted by the Common Council, on the ground that he had dissented from the grant: and his plea was actually accepted as valid.[1] If he had been absent from the Council after due summons, or had attended and kept silence, he would apparently have been held to have tacitly assented.

It would thus appear that at the beginning of the thirteenth century, the right of majorities was by no means admitted in questions of money grants, while it was only tentatively applied to other issues. The convenience of the arrangement was apparently its sole recommendation; and it was used at first only in circumstances of urgency, or in trivial matters where no influential protest was raised. There is no record from normal, peaceful times of serious opposition by a minority of any importance being overborne by mere weight of numbers. Vital issues were not, as yet, decided by a mere counting of heads. When a minority of one successfully exercised the right of refusing to pay a levy granted with absolute unanimity save for his solitary dissent, it is clear that the

[1] See McKechnie, *Magna Carta,* p. 300, and authorities there cited.

modern practice which allows no validity whatever to the protest of forty-nine men against fifty-one, was yet undreamt of.

The gradual evolution of the modern doctrine may, perhaps, be traced. At first a handful of determined or influential men could render a decision nugatory; by degrees, equality was established among the votes of all present, and a surplus of one vote came to be regarded as equally potent with an overwhelming majority. This gradual change was accompanied by another: the exceptional became the normal, and an expedient, originally confined to trivial details of convenience or procedure, was extended to embrace the most vital issues. By a bare majority of one, the House of Commons (from which all effective restraints have at last been removed) may now, without breaking any law or constitutional understanding, regulate a man's mode of life, alter the conditions on which his success in business depends, take away his property, coerce him into what he considers dishonest or irreligious conduct.

The rigour of the doctrine of majority rule was, indeed, greatly softened by the traditions of compromise that till recently formed so salutary a feature of English public life. Government by discussion has exercised a moderating effect, by preventing any one party from pushing its theories to excess. Of late years, however, partly, it may be, because the old system of government by discussion is played out, the spirit of compromise has been less conspicuous. Politicians, dependent on the support of organised bodies of constituents with definitely formulated demands, cannot afford to listen to arguments from the other side, or to abate the claims of those who keep them in power. The full pound of flesh must be ruthlessly exacted.

The increased difficulties that surround the path of compromise have resulted in the harsher operation of majority rule in recent controversies. The culminating point was reached, perhaps, with the complete failure of the Conference of 1910, held under pathetic circumstances that made a spirit of concession imperative. Not a line of the Parliament Bill of the following year was altered in deference to the scruples of the opposition. The demands of nearly half the nation were forced upon the other half in the form to which they were most violently opposed—the form dictated, word by word, by their opponents. Government by discussion, if it still exists, failed to secure alteration in any one particular. Popular government, in this instance, meant, not compromise between conflicting views, but the complete triumph of one party and the complete humiliation of the other. Nearly half the nation was powerless to resist or modify a measure they regarded with dismay. Majority rule, pushed ruthlessly to its logical issue, leaves minorities, however numerous and influential, at the mercy of a sovereign power against whose decisions there is no appeal, and to whom the possibility of compromise is increasingly difficult.

In brief, majority rule, at first tentatively introduced into England, perhaps in the thirteenth century, attained gradually an assured and, afterwards, a commanding position; its sphere has been constantly extended, while the rights of minorities have been correspondingly diminished; the earlier rule of practice, requiring large and influential majorities has been abandoned; and, finally, the tradition in favour of conciliation and compromise has fallen into abeyance. The triumph of majority rule is thus complete. An expedient, originally intended for unimportant uses, has by misleading analogies made stealthy encroachments into spheres where its operation is dangerous and inappropriate.

(2) *Justification in Logic and Expediency.*—Is it possible to justify the universal applicability of majority rule, either on grounds of philosophic principle or of utility and common sense? There are some spheres to which it is obviously inapplicable. In the conduct of war, for example, an army whose strategy was determined by the

wishes of the majority would fare badly; while diplomatic action that required confirmation by Referendum, would have few epoch-making treaties to show. It by no means follows, however, that the rule of majorities is inappropriate to all branches of legislation and statecraft.

Any serious endeavour to define its legitimate sphere of authority would probably do well to proceed from the simple to the complex, beginning with problems affecting small societies or groups of individuals, and then applying the conclusions thus suggested to the complex world of modern statecraft. All that can be attempted here is to show that there are some situations to which the application of the principle would be both dangerous and absurd, while in others it is as just as it is indispensable.

Take such an illustration as the following. Ten able-bodied seamen and a millionaire in feeble health are left, by the sinking of their vessel, adrift on a small rowing boat, far from land, with a limited stock of provisions. Some would seek safety in the West, others in the East. Here, it would be only reasonable that the votes of a majority, even of a bare majority of six to five, should settle the direction in which to steer. Soon, however, other questions are discussed: What share, if any, of the food supplies, now rapidly running out, is to be allotted to the physically useless member of the company? On what terms is he to be allowed to diminish the resources on which the safety of all depends. He is willing to pay a reasonable honorarium to the oarsmen on whose exertions he is dependent; but who is to fix the amount? The millionaire offers each seaman 10s. a day; but his companions in misfortune ask an immediate surrender of the purse he carries with him, and an I.O.U. for £100,000 to each of them—payable on reaching shore in safety. If the simple rule of majorities were here adopted, the wealthy individual would be hopelessly outvoted: the transference of the dispute from the sphere of contract to that of legislation would result in a miscarriage of justice. The wealthy individual might, however, resort to guile—to such equivalent of "lobbying" or "log-rolling" as circumstances allowed. He might sow dissension among the ten by destroying their identity of interest. Beginning in a minority of one, he offers five of the more sympathetic seamen £110,000 each (in place of £100,000), on condition that the five others get nothing. The Bill before the House, as thus amended, will save him nearly half a million, as contrasted with the earlier arrangement that stript him of all he had. Millionaires are not the only men who are liable to suffer under the rule of the majority.

It is easy to vary in imagination the

constituent factors of such suddenly created commonwealths of shipwrecked wanderers. Another isolated boat, for example, contains the captain, four able-bodied sailors, and six well-to-do passengers. Are the latter to rule the company by simply outvoting their companions? Are they justified, by the principle of majority rule, in dictating the amount of labour at the oars to be required of each? Are the minority of sailors bound to submit to "the will of the people"; or are they justified in stipulating for high remuneration from softly nurtured passengers who place a higher value on their own lives, and are well able to pay a heavy bill? Are all voices of captain, crew, and passengers to have equal weight in questions affecting the navigation of the boat?

Examples might readily be multiplied to show the absurdity, injustice, and danger of majority rule applied indiscriminately to the adjustment of the relations of individuals. A procedure, useful and necessary for deciding trivial issues or points of mere convenience, where no fundamental principles are concerned, becomes hurtful and monstrous when extended to questions of life and death, and of all that makes life dear. The consequences are the more appalling, if votes are to be taken on isolated issues, under such conditions as to assure the triumph of concrete selfish interests over abstract principles of right and wrong.[1] There is no justification, either in reason, equity, custom, or common sense for a political system which places the liberty and property, lives and honour of one-half of the community absolutely and legally at the mercy of the other half.

III. *Legal and Moral Rights of Minorities.*

There is a sharp distinction between the theory and practice of democracy. In theory, all citizens have equal rights: in practice, minorities have no effective rights at all. Minorities, as plain matter of fact, have, under a popularly elected House of Commons, no protection whatever for their legal rights. Any practical safeguards for the continuance of such rights still existing in Great Britain, such as the Lords' power of delaying certain classes of bills, are due to the fact that democracy is not yet quite complete. In the perfect democracy of the future, where political equality rules unchecked, the security and comfort of minorities (unless rooted in corruption or guile) will depend entirely on the good-will of the majority who

[1] *Cf.* Sidney Low, *Governance of England*, p. 11. "The spectacle of millions of free men in a free State, habitually governed in opposition to their own will and their own convictions, is so astonishing that we prefer to avert our gaze from it."

control the law-making machine. That majority's sense of power will be tempered only by their own generosity, or by dread of a change of fortune at the polls, putting the dog that is for the moment undermost in a position to avenge past wrongs.

It may be urged that minorities may safely count upon the moderation and good nature of their successful opponents when in power; that they have at least two rights:—the right humbly to petition their masters for justice or mercy; and the right, by persuasion or deception, to turn their minority into a majority, if they can. Further, by "log-rolling," it is possible for several minorities to combine to form a coalition majority. Such arguments are beside the point. Freedom of appeal to the generosity of others is a poor substitute for a right of one's own; while the possibility of turning the tables at some future date does not make the present position of an unprotected subject more supportable. By themselves, minorities are powerless: having no effective political rights, they have therefore no security for the continuance of their civil rights. Legally, they are rightless. On any theory of society, however, and particularly on a theory that bases itself on the abstract doctrine of equality, it is impossible to deny that all citizens have equally a moral right to protection from unjust interference. Believers in the divine right of majorities have the difficult task of justifying an anomaly that may deprive nearly half the citizens, of all effective legal rights.

The chief use of a Constitution, indeed, after providing for the establishment of order and devising efficient administrative machinery, is to protect the rights and liberties of all classes of its subjects against the abuse of power. The main interest of the long story of constitutional development in England, lies in the vicissitudes of the struggle to establish proper safeguards of individual rights against the encroachments of those entrusted with supreme power. Yet, the safeguards planned against the autocratic rule of Plantagenet or Stewart, or against the dangers incident to the mixed governments of a later day, are useless under a pure democracy. "The function of Liberalism in the past," in the opinion of Herbert Spencer, "was that of putting a limit to the power of kings. The function of true Liberalism in the future will be that of putting a limit to the power of parliaments."

What the present age requires is safeguards against the tyranny of majorities. No free constitution that does not provide these is worthy of the name. "The most certain test," says Lord Acton,[1] "by which we judge whether a country is really free is the amount of security enjoyed by minorities." Unhappily, in Great

[1] *Essays on Liberty*, p. 4.

Britain, unlike in this respect both her own Oversea Dominions and the American Commonwealth, no such safeguards exist. In what was once its most conspicuous excellence, the English Constitution has failed.

To sum up, the theory of democracy has three radical defects: its initial assumption of the political equality of beings essentially unequal is untenable; its claim for the divine right of majorities to work their will upon defeated minorities is unfounded; while its total denial of effective constitutional and legal rights to men, whose equality in moral rights forms its own root doctrine, is illogical and absurd. Democracy, founded on a basis of false and self-contradictory theory, can never in practice prove a satisfactory system of government. It is deficient in all that makes constitutional liberty and progress possible, for it is built upon the ruins of the rights of minorities.

CHAPTER VI

SAFEGUARDS AND PRACTICAL SUGGESTIONS

WHAT are the aims and ideals of modern Liberalism? Momentous as the question is—for the destiny of Great Britain depends on it—it is not easy to find an answer; no official definition of goal or methods is available.

In marked contrast to the *laissez faire* and individualist programme of the Liberalism of last century, the Liberalism of to-day is content to rest upon unformulated principles, as vague as they are far-reaching. No scientific writer, acknowledged as its prophet, has arisen to place a reasoned statement of the aims of modern Liberalism, or of their philosophic justification, before the world. The explanation is not hard to find: the leaders of modern Liberalism are not agreed on fundamental principles. Vital differences exist, and the party sways in one direction or the other, according to the changing vicissitudes of the hour.

One group of Liberals is content to share

its main constitutional ideals with the bulk of moderate Conservatists: another group favours a policy the results of which can with difficulty be distinguished from Socialism or at best from the closely allied Collectivism. The all-important question not only for Liberals, but for the entire nation, is which of these two sections will prevail; for on that depends the future of Great Britain. Hence, definition of the standpoint, policy, and underlying principles of modern Liberalism is the crying necessity of the day.

I. *The Need of Definition.*

What guiding principles should direct and limit the policy of reformers in their philanthropic efforts to effect by means of legislation a more equitable distribution of the comforts of life between rich and poor? On what principles, other than mere electioneering expediency, are the objects of new taxation to be selected and the amount determined? Is it not possible, by the issue of a definite Liberal Confession of Faith, to convince reasonable Conservatives that a genuine distinction does exist between the Liberalism that would force the unwilling rich to make a moderate contribution to the needs of their less fortunate fellow-citizens, and the Socialism that aims at the ultimate extinction of all forms of private wealth?

Upon what principles (to approach the problem from its other side) are the just demands of labour to be estimated? Are the organised workers to be placed in uncontrolled command of a legislature, empowered to fix wages and hours of labour; or, is it possible to place the decision in neutral and unprejudiced hands?

Amid the bitter party strife of recent years there has been danger of forgetting that the points separating moderate Liberal from moderate Conservative are as nothing compared with the gulf that separates both from the revolutionary who is deliberately moving towards the goal of Socialism. Yet to some small extent, for the immediate future, Liberal and Socialist will walk side by side. It is the more necessary that the former should realise the exact point at which their paths diverge;[1] and when he has satisfied himself on this matter, he will help to restore confidence by making the result of his deliberations public. It is impossible to forecast how soon Liberals and Conservatives may be forced to combine in opposition to the attempts of Syndicalism and other malign forces threatening to engulf society; and, in view of such necessity, it is a duty to do what

[1] There is an old saying, sometimes attributed to Cromwell, that "no one goes so far as the man who doesn't know where he is going." Cited by Dicey, *Law and Opinion*, p. 230.

is possible, to remove misconceptions and mutual suspicions.

The classes who place a higher value on stability than on progress will more readily acquiesce in moderate reforms, if they know where the line is to be drawn, or if they even know that a line will be drawn somewhere, before Niagara is reached. The classes who have suffered most from the burden of increased taxation will bear their heavy losses with more equanimity, if they realise the point at which Liberal and Socialist ideals diverge. Even owners of real estate might recover confidence in the justice of the Legislature, if Liberalism officially dissociated itself from the doctrine of the "Single Tax," and repudiated all sympathy with a policy of gradually confiscating land values to the State.

A first duty of Liberalism—urged alike by prudence and magnanimity—would thus seem to be to allay suspicion by the promulgation of an authoritative statement of its attitude towards property. It is incumbent upon Liberal leaders to show wherein Liberal finance differs from Communistic confiscation; to formulate principles that justify the one and yet allow the condemnation of the other. If moderate men receive satisfactory assurance that the institution of private property (still considered by many to be a main bulwark of the State) is as safe under a

Liberal as under a Conservative Ministry, then much will have been done to restore the economic security presupposed in national well-being.

It is merely another side of the same requirement that the leaders of the new democracy should endeavour to devise a sound scheme of national finance, based on the advice of experts rather than on the vicissitudes of party politics, or the likes and dislikes of party leaders. The burden of national expenditure ought to be borne by the various factors that make up the nation, on principles of equity and science, and lifted altogether out of the region of party.

Finally, if any element of truth lurks in the assertion that democratic legislation discourages self-denial and accustoms the masses to look for State-help in place of helping themselves, it is a pressing duty of statesmen of all parties to devise an antidote to these cankering evils. In aiming at a rapid realisation of the poor man's paradise that is the dream of reformers, there must be kept in view the possibility of creating, in the not distant future, a universal poor man's purgatory. A democracy of the morally, mentally, and physically debased, presents a prospect that is not attractive. In this respect, Socialist reformers have an advantage over Liberal democrats, for the Socialists have far-reaching schemes for controlling the birth-rate and the family in the supposed interests of Eugenics.

They recognise that a pampering government must guard the gates of population. Well-meaning Liberal philanthropists must bethink them how far it is possible to adopt one part of the Socialist programme without accepting the whole; and whether they are not, in their good nature, being misled into unknown dangers by beginning at the wrong end. On these and other grounds, definition is urgently required.

A mere formal declaration of Liberal policy might do much to allay the fears that at present render uneasy all those who have anything to lose; diminish the steady emigrant flow of capital and enterprise to less democratic countries; and help to restore, in some measure, the sense of security on which economic well-being depends. Liberal reformers and Conservative social democrats would do well to revise their attitude towards democracy, to consider how far in the ideal commonwealth it must be tempered by the introduction of other elements.

II. *Modification of Democratic Theory.*

Vox populi does not contain the sum total of political wisdom. The people need something more than the immediate gratification of momentarily changing desires, something more than untrammelled opportunity of doing what is right in their own eyes. They need, among other things, expert scientific guidance in specialised fields of knowledge. They need protection from unscrupulous political quacks and servile flatterers. They need opportunities for calm reflection. They need to be guarded against their own ignorance and rashness, which unaided might lead them to irremediable disaster. They need, by the removal of temptation, to be guarded against themselves and their own lower appetites: to be guided along the path of justice, on which alone continued national prosperity is to be found.

The needs of minorities are even greater, for they require protection from the extreme consequences of a doctrine of unqualified democratic equality. Minorities, even justly unpopular minorities, have right to some measure of protection for themselves and their belongings, against the crushing despotism of majorities. Thus, in a democratic state, constitutional safeguards are as necessary as under any other form of government. In some respects, more so; for it is easier for the public opinion of the many to act as a drag on the tyranny of the few, than for the few to restrain the many.

Safeguards are, in particular, needed against the well-meaning extravagance of a philanthropic but ignorant House of Commons. Something is needed to take the place of the ancient checks and balances that have been destroyed. Some new device is urgently required to restore government by free discussion to its ancient throne. A firm constitutional framework is, indeed, more than ever necessary in a state of society, where no limits are recognised to the province of legislation, and no natural rights of individuals are allowed to bar the free gratification of the desires of majorities.

It is possible to argue that no mere constitutional machinery could afford efficient protection. Legal restraints are likely to prove bonds of paper, if unaccompanied by the moral qualities that enforce them, and by the spirit of compromise and watchfulness that recognises, in an invasion of the rights of one man, an invasion of the rights of all. If public opinion and respect for the spirit of the constitution do not actively support the safeguards contained in legal documents, these are likely to prove mere dead letters. The electors need, for their own good and that of the commonwealth, education in the principles of political science; they urgently need to be taught to look beyond the immediate objects of party controversy and of individual wants.

Constitutional restraints, without an enlightened sense of citizenship, are thus far from being the whole solution; but they are one essential element in that solution. Further, their mere existence helps to induce in the nation a more equitable frame of mind. It is not by destroying the legal bulwarks of individual liberty that a spirit of freedom is cultivated in a nation. In Great Britain, however, these bulwarks have, by a gradual process only recently completed (or perhaps still incomplete), been slowly undermined. The position of modern England in this respect, may be illustrated by comparison, not only with England in the past, but with the other progressive nations that are its rivals in commerce and in the struggle for empire.

III. *Constitutional Safeguards in Foreign Countries.*

Great Britain, still nominally under a monarchic form of government, approaches in actual practice an absolute democracy, more nearly than is the case in the United States of America, or perhaps in any of the republics of the world. The American Commonwealth has not one but several distinct constitutional expedients for protecting the rights of minorities, and presents a marked contrast to the conditions that prevail in England, under the unrestrained omnipotence of a one-chambered Parliament.

American safeguards of minority rights have already been mentioned;[1] but, at a time when

[1] See *supra*, p. 59, 60.

the old Constitution of Great Britain has been thrown into the melting pot, the eyes of Englishmen naturally turn to the expedients adopted in the great Anglo-Saxon democratic nation as a protection for the rights of minorities. Furnishing analogies that might possibly be applied to English institutions, these American safeguards of constitutional rights would seem to call for a somewhat fuller exposition. These safeguards, as already explained, are five in number.

(1) The mere existence of a written Constitution raises a series of barriers to restrict the ascendency of the many over the few. Fundamental principles, on the faith of which obligations have been undertaken, money invested, and businesses built up, cannot be suddenly upset by the insertion of a few words in an ordinary act of the Legislature, as may be done in England. Under any form of written Constitution, individuals are sure of, at least, a few fixed cities of refuge that cannot be engulfed by revolutionary legislation.

(2) The framework of government in the United States, however, has been specially careful of the constitutional liberty of individuals. The number of topics upon which Congress can legislate has been strictly curtailed.

(3) Minorities and the rights of property are

further protected by the existence of a Second Chamber, with far wider powers than the House of Lords possesses even in theory, and enjoying the popular support that enables it fearlessly to use its legal powers unchallenged. Unsettling legislation, ordinary or financial, even if within the powers of the Federal Congress, has thus to run the gauntlet of two equally powerful Chambers, before it passes into law.

(4) The fourth of the American constitutional safeguards lies in the division of supreme power between the federal authorities and those of the various individual states. The menaced individual is not left at the absolute mercy of the central tyrant. The local Legislature stands as a buffer between them; no one absolutely omnipotent dictator holds undisputed sway.

(5) Lastly, the separation of executive from legislative authority acts as an additional safeguard of individual liberties in America. The conditions are the exact reverse of those prevailing in Great Britain. The President of the United States, within his proper sphere, has equal authority with Congress, to which he is not responsible.

If the President desires to change the law in order to invade the liberty or confiscate the property of any class or group of citizens, he can accomplish this only by argument or persuasion; not, as may be done in England, by the mere issue of orders, enforced on a regimented majority by the party Whips. Congress is quite at liberty to discuss, with open mind, the underlying principles of the changes proposed, and to reject them—without incurring any penalty—if they seem hurtful to the best interests of the commonwealth. The American President, unlike the British Cabinet, by no means carries the legislature in his pocket; the House of Representatives is as likely as not to refuse consent to measures dictated by electioneering motives, while the Senate is a powerful body not to be cowed into accepting changes it knows to be unjust or inexpedient. In particular, the President cannot introduce, on his own authority, changes in the principles of taxation entailing special hardship on the more prominent of his political opponents. He must use the weapons allowed him by existing statutes, for he cannot alter the law to give free play to his desires of vengeance, or to increase his chances of securing election for a new term of office.

In addition to sharing in the protection afforded by these five powerful safeguards, all of a perfectly legal nature, wealth in the United States finds means of making its weight felt by a sixth expedient more effective than creditable. In opposition to the brute voting power of numbers, wealth has found in America illicit means to redress by guile the balance in its own favour. The practice of "lobbying" is unfortunately too well known to call for more than a passing notice. Large sums of money are sometimes accumulated by wealthy trusts and corporations for the purpose of facilitating legislation favourable to private interests. Deplorable as such methods are, and foreign to the present spirit of British politics, it may be worth while to pause and consider whether something of the same kind is not likely to assert itself as a necessary counteraction in all nations, where majorities subject minorities to their unjust will.

In an ideal commonwealth, all legitimate forms of power, moral, intellectual, or physical, ought to find their natural expression through constitutional organs, and ought to exercise their natural influence on the national destinies. If any one element is unduly depressed, an artificial condition is established; the pent-up energy, dammed back in one direction, will escape in another. The force of majorities that refuse to lend ear to the entreaties or arguments of opponents, will tend to be counteracted by the guile of minorities.

IV. *Suggested Safeguards for Great Britain.*

If the American Commonwealth has not escaped the vices and dangers of democracy in spite of the five powerful safeguards devised against them by the framers of its Constitution, Great Britain, moving rapidly towards a democracy more thorough-going and totally without any such constitutional bulwarks, is faced with a serious problem. She has to determine to what extent, if at all, minorities ought to be protected, and to devise expedients for effecting this without an undue sacrifice of the legitimate ideals of democracy.

Great Britain has to find antidotes for the dangers inherent in that popular government to which she is irretrievably committed. Lord Acton[1] shows that a consensus of opinion holds these dangers and vices to be neither few nor unimportant. All the classical writers on that great theme—Tocqueville, Calhoun, Mill, and Laboulaye—he points out, "have shown democracy without respect for the past or care for the future, regardless of public faith and of national honour, extravagant and inconstant, jealous of talent and of knowledge, indifferent to justice but servile towards opinion, incapable of organisation, impatient of authority, averse from

[1] *Essays on Liberty*, p. 93.

obedience, hostile to religion and to established law." If this picture is too dark, it yet contains a useful warning that the millenium may not be immediately established by the mere abolition of all remnants of monarchic and aristocratic authority.

Would it be possible, and if so, would it be desirable that this country should adopt constitutional safeguards on the lines of those of the American system of government, which so materially check, without altogether eradicating, the evils inherent in democracy? Of these, the most effective is undoubtedly the existence of a strong and popular Second Chamber, supported by public opinion, and putting into constant use the extensive powers secured to it by law over ordinary and financial legislation. It is obvious that, whatever lessons may yet be learned in the school of experience, the present state of political opinion in this country would not tolerate any attempt to emulate, in this matter of a strong Second Chamber, the constitutional phenomena of the great Republic, which is the home of Anglo-Saxon democracy.

The sole object for which a written Constitution has yet been even tentatively suggested in Great Britain has been to define and thereby to curtail the power of the Upper Chamber. The Parliament Act of 1911 may be said to be the outcome of this suggestion. It is not, indeed, a written constitutional code, perhaps not even a fragment of such a code. Its professed aim was not to innovate, but merely to transfer certain accepted principles from the region of conventional understanding into that of statute law; and it thus exhibits some features in common with the written Constitutions of countries possessing codes. The object of the Parliament Bill, however, in marked contrast to the American and other similar codes, was not to protect the rights of minorities against the tyranny of the popularly elected chamber, but rather to deprive them of these rights entirely.

At the present moment, in England, refuge from the possible excesses of democracy is not to be sought either in the direction of a strong Second Chamber, or of fundamental rights guaranteed by a written Constitution. Is it possible, then, that it is towards federalism of one kind or another, that minorities in England, Scotland, or Ireland must look for protection in the future? "Of all the checks on democracy," in Lord Acton's opinion,[1] "federalism has been the most efficacious and the most congenial." "It affords," he adds, "the strongest basis for a Second Chamber, which has been found the essential security for freedom in any genuine democracy." Even to those who neither believe in Second Chambers nor distrust democracies,

[1] *Essays on Liberty*, p. 98.

federalism may well make strong appeal. Whether the grant to Ireland of a Constitution on the colonial model is really a step towards the federation of what men have been accustomed, by a century's usage, to call the United Kingdom, is open to doubt; but federal schemes are undoubtedly in the air.

It seems hardly possible for the most philanthropic of British Governments to put Scotland and Wales in the same favoured position as Ireland, which is to have the exclusive right to manage its own affairs, to hold the casting vote in determining English and Imperial affairs, and to be paid handsomely for accepting this position. The Government making these generous provisions has grown accustomed, it is true, to finance its schemes from the purses of its opponents; but there are limits to the resources of even the most princely generosity. Under normal conditions, each federal unit of a federated Great Britain would require to pay its own way. It is not practicable that each province should receive more from the Imperial Exchequer than it contributes.

The main gain, however, expected from a readjustment of the Constitution on a federal basis, is a gain in the freedom of minorities. Even if the legislatures of the constituent communities were composed only of single-chambers, some measure of protection, it is hoped, would yet be afforded by the splitting up of power between the central and the local parliaments. Federalism within the British Isles would seem to be still a matter of the distant future. Public opinion is not ripe for it; and in view of the predominance of England, it is difficult to conceive a scheme at once practicable and symmetrical.

The remaining expedient is even less likely to be adopted here, where the Cabinet system has struck deep root. When the American Constitution was framed, the doctrine of the distribution of powers was considered the main protection of the subjects' liberties against the tyranny of authority. President and Congress were made co-ordinate, and ministerial responsibility was deliberately discarded. The American citizen, governed by two independent authorities, is never absolutely at the mercy of either. It is impossible to adopt such a safeguard in England, where all power is focussed in the small knot of men who, as the acknowledged leaders of their party, exercise absolute control over both administrative and legislative machinery.

In Great Britain, then, all the old checks and balances have ceased to act. The prerogatives of the monarch go to swell the powers of the Cabinet: the once co-ordinate authority of the Lords is reduced to a right of delay or obstruction. The House of Commons merely registers the presumed will of the majority as interpreted by the party leaders. No written Constitution exists to guarantee fundamental principles. Nothing is sacred from the dominating authority of an Act of Parliament, and no bills but the Cabinet's bills have any chance of becoming laws. Not one of the constitutional safeguards, devised by the wisdom of centuries against the dangers of an earlier state of society, is of any avail under the changed conditions of to-day. In all these respects, the contrast with the United States is absolute. Citizens of the great republic live to-day under a Constitution which is in full working order, popular, and respected, while the far-famed British system of government would seem to have suffered shipwreck.

V. *Suggested Safeguards, continued—the Referendum and Proportional Representation.*

It is to democratic Switzerland rather than to democratic America, however, that Great Britain, now that her old constitutional bulwarks have decayed, seems to be turning in search of new ones. The Referendum, which not long ago attracted the favourable notice of

Liberals, has now been repudiated by them and adopted by Conservatives. An expedient which, in the face of much difference of opinion, has been found possible in a small, homogeneous, and federal republic, whose territories are compactly knit together, has been suggested as suitable for a non-federal World-Empire, governing peoples of alien race in every continent of the globe.

The great merit claimed for the Referendum, is that it is thoroughly democratic in its tendencies and results. The claim is one that cannot be gainsaid; it is of such a nature, however, as not specially to allay the fears of those who question the complete wisdom, reasonableness, and justice of democracy, as an ideal form of government. If the Referendum is, in its very essence, democratic, it is more likely to intensify than to abate the dangers of democracy. If the chief want of our present system, or absence of system, is a safeguard of minority rights, that is not to be found in the expedient of submitting individual questions, as they arise, to the determination of majorities. The more extensively the Referendum is resorted to, the more complete will be the triumph of democracy.

Most advocates of that fashionable remedy, indeed, would seem to assume the possibility of confining it to the specific issues to which they personally desire to apply it. They contemplate its use in rare and isolated crises of politics, where other remedies have failed. They imagine that the mass of voters, having become accustomed to be consulted on the issues that particularly interest constitutional theorists, will not demand increasingly to be consulted also on the issues that particularly interest themselves.

The experience of Switzerland, the home of the Referendum, should not be ignored. Not only has the sphere of the Referendum been steadily extended, but it has brought in its train that potent engine of democracy, known as the Initiative—an expedient under which any measure, however unwise, unjust, or ill-drafted, that has obtained the necessary number of signatures must (whether the Government be willing or no) be referred to the decision of the people. Such a bill, accepted by a majority, straightway becomes a statute, in face even of the determined and united opposition of both legislative chambers. The Initiative is the apotheosis of democracy. It may be urged, in theory, that it is possible to have the Referendum without the Initiative; but recent history shows that, if the one expedient is conceded, the adoption of the other is merely a matter of time. Such has been the experience of Switzerland; and the American evidence points in the same direction.

This is not the place to discuss the other

difficulties connected with the practical working of the Referendum[1]; sufficient has, perhaps, been said to show that to accept it as an adequate protection for the rights of minorities is a counsel of despair. A one-sided argument in its favour might be attempted on the ground that any remedy is better than none: that under a regime where the supreme Executive and the supreme Legislature, instead of balancing each other, are united in a dominant Cabinet, the interposition of a direct popular vote between that Cabinet and its victims affords some measure of security.

The answer is twofold. Even if the Referendum partially accomplished what its friends expected, this would be at an expense disproportionate to the gain. Further, the security is delusive; if it saved minorities from tyranny in a few instances, in which the leaders of the party in power did not really represent the popular will, it would ultimately hand these same minorities over to a more complete subserviency to their real taskmasters, the majority in whose name the Government acts.

Considered as a substitute for an effective Second Chamber, the Referendum cannot be accepted. It affords no real, permanent protection for minorities; but, in an industrial

[1] See *Edinburgh Review,* January 1910, and my *Reform of the House of Lords,* Chap. VIII.

country, would rather make their bondage more complete. In its essential nature it is merely an appeal from numbers reckoned on one system to numbers reckoned on another, and from the decision of the masses on mixed issues to their decision on a series of nominally separate issues. The more nearly it approached its own ideals, the more deadly would it become. Yet, where, logically, can we draw the line? If one group of questions is to be referred direct to the electors, why not all?

Imagine, for a moment, how the Referendum, universally applied, would work in actual practice. How would the electors answer the following three questions, if these were separately referred to them? When coal-mines are nationalised, ought the nation to buy at a fair market value, or make no payment at all? Is it your will that all incomes over £1000 should be forfeited to the Exchequer and divided among wage-earners? Do you approve of an addition of five shillings a week to the present remuneration of wage-earners of all classes?

These are extreme instances, doubtless, not likely ever to be made the subject-matter of an actual Referendum. There are many other isolated issues, however, which could not be placed before the electors without grave danger. The narrower the limits within which the

Referendum is confined, the better will it be for the rights of minorities. It is for its advocates to satisfy themselves that, once it has been introduced, it will be possible to prevent its extension to new fields.

In thus rejecting the Referendum as a panacea for present maladies, it should be clearly understood that its chief dangers are common to all forms, aspects, and expedients of democracy. It contains the concentrated essence of democracy: that is all. This very fact renders it the more remarkable, that a party which claims to represent the people should have refused to accept this most effective method of giving effect to that people's will. In discarding the Referendum, Liberals are tacitly repudiating, along with it, their profession of belief in the principles of an absolute democracy.

The safeguards of individual liberty, sought by some reformers in the Referendum, are found by others in proportional representation. It is claimed for this vaunted remedy for the evils of our party system that it would secure the proper representation of minorities. If a five-member constituency returned three Conservatives and two Liberals, it is obvious that every Liberal elector might extract such pleasure as he could from the fact that, while his "members" will among them cast one effective vote against every measure he holds dear, he is still represented, in a sense, by the two who are habitually outvoted. Under such a system, further, majorities will tend to be smaller and also less compact. The tyranny of majorities may thus, in some measure, be modified; but it will not be removed. Minorities would still be liable to have their lives regulated and their goods confiscated by their successful opponents. The adherents of proportional representation have still to satisfy the public that any one of their numerous schemes will render the existence of an efficient Second Chamber unnecessary as a safeguard of individual liberties.

VI. *Suggested Safeguards, continued—Second Chambers and Councils of Experts.*

New-fangled devices thus fail to provide the needed safeguards; and yet English reformers are unwilling to fall back on so antiquated and commonplace an expedient as that which commends itself to the other fully civilised countries of the world, and to all of the British self-governing colonies, namely, the requirement that no bill shall become law without obtaining the consent of two co-ordinate chambers, constituted upon different principles. This bicameral system, indeed, is not under all circumstances an adequate protection for minorities; but it is better than none.

A conclusion so humdrum and uninspiring, to an age that loves novelties and dangerous experiments, by no means implies that the old House of Lords, unaltered in composition, ought to have its ancient powers restored. That House had long ceased to be a sufficient protection against hurtful legislation. Its authority had been gradually curtailed till, long before the Parliament Act of 1911 dealt it a knock-down blow, it had reached a lower level than any Second Chamber of a continental nation of the first rank. Its permanent continuance on an unreformed basis had become impossible, because of its unequal operation against objectionable bills of Liberals and Conservatives respectively. This was not only galling and unfair; but it led directly to a diminution in the moral weight of the Upper House, and rendered it impotent to use any of its powers without arousing threats of revolutionary violence.

Unpopular and discredited, the Second Chamber proved useless, for example, in guarding the nation from the anticipated evils of the Trade Disputes Act; and the Conservative Upper House is now frequently denounced as sharing the guilt of the Liberal Government, which forced that bill through, in spite of the consensus of moderate opinion against it. What is wanted is a powerful Second Chamber, like the American Senate or the South African Upper House, deeply rooted in the affections of all classes, composed of moderate men of both parties in equal numbers, dealing out even-handed justice to the ill-digested measures of Cabinets of all political complexions, and abundantly able to protect society from hurtful legislation. A Second Chamber, which is only a gilded sham, with nominal powers intended for ornament and not for use, is worse than no Second Chamber at all.

It is unlikely, however, that even if an English counterpart of the American Senate were established with real power over ordinary legislation, it would be allowed any appreciable share in the control of Bills of Supply. Such control, if pushed to excess, would subject the executive power in Great Britain to two masters, which might issue two sets of orders inconsistent with each other. The necessary supplies might be denied by the First Chamber, unless the Executive moved in one direction; by the Second Chamber, unless it moved in the other. The electors of the United States of America accept cheerfully the prospect of such a dead-lock as a theoretical possibility rather than a practical likelihood; but English politicians, trained under the Cabinet system, would probably be less complacent.

If the remodelled House of Lords, in contrast

with the Upper Chambers of Canada, Australia, and South Africa, is allowed no effective control over the national expenditure, it will be necessary to provide safeguards of a different kind. As to the nature and even the possibility of these, opinion is likely to be sharply divided. The first essential, however, would clearly be the institution of a tribunal possessing the confidence of both parties, competent to decide on what constitutes a Money Bill, thus relieving the Speaker of a difficult and invidious duty thrust on him by the Parliament Act. Almost equally desirable would be the recognition of the need for a differentiation in parliamentary procedure in matters of supply, and in matters of ways and means respectively. Over the latter, the Second Chamber ought clearly to exercise fuller powers than over the former. If Bills of Supply are placed under the Commons' exclusive control, the Executive is assured of the financial support necessary for carrying on the King's Government. The guardians of minorities might with comparative security withdraw any claim to concur in the appropriation of public money, if the need of their consent were clearly recognised to all new charges to be laid on the classes of tax-payers with whose interests they were more closely associated.

Even such a scheme as this, unlikely as it would be to find favour with expectant beneficiaries of the public bounty, would afford insufficient security against the philanthropic enthusiasm of the framers of modern Utopias, placed in power by the acclamations of the populace. Hence, further expedients of the nature of safeguards would have to be devised. With this object in view, one practical suggestion, which would seem to lie outside the region of party warfare, may here be hazarded as probably of value either taken by itself, or in conjunction with the other measures already discussed. This expedient may be provisionally described as the appointment of an advisory council of non-political financial experts, to advise but not to control the Treasury Board and Cabinet in framing their financial policy. The absolute control over the wealth of the British Empire is much too great a trust to be committed to the decision of a Cabinet raised to power by a majority on an admittedly controversial basis. It is much too great a trust to be committed, as under certain circumstances it is not impossible that it might be, to the decision of one individual, however wise, disinterested, and unbiassed.

The Treasury Board, which in theory is still responsible for guarding and replenishing the national Exchequer, is now admittedly, for all but trivial purposes, an imaginary Board; its great powers have fallen into the hands of one of its five members, the Chancellor of the Exchequer. That official has no legal power to coerce the Cabinet to adopt his financial programmes; but his opinion, as practically sole Minister of Finance, carries enormous weight.

Any statesman, therefore, who would set himself to frame a new Constitution, or remodel the old one by providing new constitutional safeguards for oppressed minorities, must provide for the possible contingency of one man's will being for the moment supreme over the financial policy of the Empire. The danger and absurdity of permitting such a dictatorship, are not lessened by the processes that determine the elevation to power of successive holders of this office. Occupying what is essentially a judicial position through his power of redistributing under legislative sanction the national revenue and capital, the Chancellor of Exchequer is not required by law to possess any of the qualifications of ordinary judges with more limited jurisdictions. Indeed, he is not required by law to possess any scientific knowledge either of the principles of administering justice or of sound finance.

His position, in actual practice, is gained as the result of a scramble in the game of politics. It is open to any aspirant who, by eloquence of an appropriate kind, gains the ear of the multitude. Our working Constitution, instead of making provision that the office should be held by a specialist in finance who is certain to be uninfluenced by party passion, makes it impossible for anyone to become Chancellor who has not, in a high degree, gifts which are unlikely to be compatible either with a mastery of the mysteries of finance, or with the possession of the calm judicial temper of compromise and moderation.

An autocrat who held office for life, the once admired benevolent despot of other days, had at least one point in his favour. He was free to carry out measures of reform on the lines suggested by scientific experts, without courting the suffrages of various sections of the electorate. The despot chosen by the people, on the contrary, though absolute while their favour lasts, is in constant fear that such favour may prove fickle. He uses his portentous powers, with one eye fixed on the national welfare, and the other roving hither and thither in the search for votes. There is little room for dubiety as to which type of autocrat is the more dangerous.

The mere possibility that a Chancellor of the Exchequer may share the people's ignorance of economic laws, makes plain to common prudence the necessity for devising an effective means of supplying the deficiency. The plan already briefly suggested may be worth the consideration of those who object on principle to all Second Chambers, as well as of those who favour them. An advisory council (to go somewhat further into details), with the legal right to be consulted by the Treasury Board and to give advice upon all financial schemes, but without any powers of enforcing its opinions, might be appointed under statutory authority. The number and qualifications of members of this body, with the rules ensuring the communication of information in sufficient time to make realities of their rights of criticism, remonstrance, and protest, would be defined in the statute creating the council. The Chancellor of Exchequer would be bound to make public, not only his own arguments and opinions, but also those of the committee. The members would be men who were not engaged in politics on either side. They might be nominated on the lines familiar in the case of royal commissions, but either for life or for definite periods of office. Their qualifications would be carefully defined. Membership would be confined to financial and scientific experts with long practical experience, men of acknowledged theoretical eminence, or holders of high official positions.

A small non-partisan body of this nature, composed of men of scientific standing and acknowleged impartiality, if unanimous in their opinion, would be influential in moderating the extreme views of successive Treasury Boards, and also in moulding public opinion. The most optimistic of Chancellors would hardly persevere in unsound finance in face of their united protest. Some measure of protection would be afforded even the most unpopular or the most helpless of minorities. On the other hand, the support of such a body would lighten the Chancellor's burden, without relieving him of ultimate responsibility. The Cabinet would be free to take the risk of proceeding with its measures, even in the face of a unanimous condemnation; but the electors, in forming an estimate of the wisdom of the Cabinet's conduct, would not be left entirely to the guidance of their own ignorance.

If opinion within the Advisory Committee were anything like equally divided, a Chancellor of the Exchequer, equipped with the power of ingenious rhetoric rather than financial knowledge, would have little difficulty in explaining from numerous platforms that the expert verdict was really entirely in favour of his latest scheme.

This mild, non-political, checking machinery would not place an undue restraint on the just and reasonable schemes of the most sanguine of Chancellors, who would still be left in possession of sufficiently wide influence for the legitimate furtherance of his own schemes of a charitable or political nature. On the other hand, those minorities who are now without right of appeal against even the most monstrous invasions of their cherished liberties, would benefit from the Cabinet's unwillingness to force upon the country schemes, that had received the strong condemnation of a body of eminent economists, appointed under Act of Parliament, and drawn from the moderate and judicially-minded experts of all shades of political opinion.[1]

1 To the kindness of Mr John Murray, the author is indebted for a valuable suggestion which reached him, unfortunately, too late to be discussed in the text. Mr Murray, convinced of the need for devising new constitutional safeguards to take the place of those that have been ruthlessly demolished, suggests that if the House of Commons were to adopt the expedient of voting by ballot in the Committee-stage of all important bills, the injurious tyranny of the Whips would be greatly curtailed and, in some cases at least, Members would be free to vote according to their consciences. This would ensure a more honest discussion of complicated bills, would make the Government of the day more cautious, and would blunt the edge of the "guillotine." Mr Murray realises the practical difficulty of reconciling such an innovation with the requirements of the party system in its present form, even if existing conventions of the Constitution could be so altered as to make it clear that a defeat in Committee—or even a series of defeats—would not involve the resignation of the Government. As the whole book was already in type when these suggestions reached the author, it has not been possible to elaborate points of detail, or to discuss the best method of overcoming the practical difficulties that would have to be faced.

VII. *Conclusion: Need of Looking Ahead.*

It is not the object of this book to insist on any special remedies, however feasible they may appear, for the evils of democracy. No cut-and-dried scheme of reconstruction is here aimed at; no condemnation of special measures of reform insisted on. The object has rather been to call for a timely consideration of modern legislative tendencies, and for a searching examination into the fundamental principles involved.

It would be impossible, even if it were desirable, for Great Britain to retrace her steps towards the ideals of a by-gone age, or to revive exploded conceptions of the narrow sphere of legitimate legislation; but there may be wisdom in inquiring as to the nature and position of rocks ahead, and in considering whether both of the great parties in the State have not acquiesced too unguardedly in a policy of drifting with the currents that set in the direction of the people's will, without due consideration for the higher principle of the people's good. If any stemming of the tide is to be accomplished, the attempt must not be long delayed. It is easier to give power to a giant than to take it back. In Bagehot's graphic words, even more noteworthy to-day than when they were first written:—"A democracy will never, save after an awful catastrophe, return what has once been conceded to it, for to do so would be to admit an inferiority in itself, of which, except by some almost unbearable misfortune, it could never be convinced."

It may not yet be too late to profit by this warning, if only the danger is realised before the avalanche of democracy has gathered sufficient momentum to defy all attempts to bar its further progress. If constitutional barriers can still be devised, they ought to be devised at once. An inquiry into the measures which are now being taken with this end in view has nothing of a cheerful nature to reveal. The Conservatives are bent on providing democracy with a new and potent weapon, by conferring on the masses the right to be directly consulted on each important issue that arises; while the Liberals are carefully eliminating any shadowy remnant of the factors that once helped to counteract the omnipotence of mere numbers.

The Referendum, abolition of plural voting, and universal franchise, among them, will add increased momentum to the moving avalanche sufficient to bring it swiftly and inevitably to the brink of the precipice. Meanwhile, democracy by no means stands idly by. While its friends of both parties work for it, it is well able to work for itself. It has, of recent years, forged new weapons, namely, the theory of Syndicalism and the practical method of the general strike, of which the nation has recently experienced some mild foretastes.

The corporate nation, it is true, against which Syndicalism makes war, if only left free to use its own resources and not prejudiced by pernicious legislation, conferring unwise privileges on those who attack it, is still able to protect itself from the effects of a general strike. Unfortunately, however, the same trade unions whose members seek to enter on a death struggle with their fellow-citizens, are learning to look with confidence to the support of a sympathetic, if not subservient, Parliament. If organised labour is able to obtain from Parliament legal powers that paralyse the arm of the community acting in its own defence, the community must go to the wall. If, outside of Parliament, numerical majorities are henceforth to push their claims by violence, and are, at the same time, to be allowed to obtain undisputed control of the machinery of legislation, the forces making for unlimited democracy in Great Britain are likely, in the near future, to move with a relentless swiftness of which the world has hitherto had no experience.

INDEX